Detroit Studies in Music Bibliography

Editor

J. Bunker Clark   University of Kansas

Music

in the

Royal Society of London

1660-1806

by

L<small>ETA</small> M<small>ILLER</small>

and

A<small>LBERT</small> C<small>OHEN</small>

DETROIT STUDIES IN MUSIC BIBLIOGRAPHY   NUMBER FIFTY-SIX
INFORMATION COORDINATORS   1987   DETROIT

Copyright © 1987 by Leta E. Miller and Albert Cohen

Printed and bound in the United States of America
Published by
Information Coordinators, Inc.
1435-37 Randolph Street
Detroit, Michigan 48226

Editing by J. Bunker Clark
Book design by Nicholas Jakubiak

Library of Congress Cataloging in Publication Data

Miller, Leta E.
    Music in the Royal Society of London, 1660-1806.

    (Detroit studies in music bibliography ; no. 56)
    Bibliography: p.
    Includes indexes.
    1. Royal Society (Great Britain) — Catalogs.
2. Music — Bibliography — Catalogs.   I. Cohen, Albert,
1929-   II. Title.   III. Series.
ML136.L8R745   1987   016.78   87-344
ISBN 0-89990-032-1

CONTENTS

LIST OF PLATES

ABBREVIATIONS

*(Complete references for printed items,
other than commonly available dictionaries and encyclopedias,
are given in the bibliography.)*

AC: J. A. Venn, *Alumni Cantabrigiensis*

Alli: Samuel Austin Allibone, *A Critical Dictionary of English Literature and British and American Authors*

Arm: W. H. G. Armytage, "The Royal Society and the Apothecaries"

BA: Howard Colvin, *A Biographical Dictionary of British Architects, 1600-1840*

Bir: Thomas Birch, *History of the Royal Society of London*

BL: Boyle Letters

BLC: British Library Catalogue of Printed Books

BP: Boyle Papers

Brit: *Encyclopedia Britannica*

Bull: Bulloch's Roll (Ms. listing of R. S. Fellows in the R.S. Library)

C: Max Caspar, *Kepler*

CP: Classified Papers

DHF: *Dictionnaire historique de la France*

DIB: John Crone, *A Concise Dictionary of Irish Biography*

DNB: *Dictionary of National Biography*

DSB: *Dictionary of Scientific Biography*

Ed.:   Edited version

EI: *Enciclopedia italiana*

EL: Early Letters

Engl. ed.: English edition

EUI: *Enciclopedia universal ilustrada*

Fos: Joseph Foster, *Alumni Oxonienses*

FRS: Fellow of the Royal Society (usually followed by date of admission)

GDEL: *Grand dictionnaire encyclopédique Larousse*

GEC Bar: G. E. Cokayne, *Complete Baronetage*

Gent M: *Gentleman's Magazine*

GLE: *Grand Larousse encyclopédique*

GM: General Manuscripts

Gun.: R. W. T. Gunther, *Early Science in Oxford*

H: Joseph Haydn, *The Book of Dignities*

Hal: *Correspondence and Papers of Edmond [sic] Halley*, ed. Eugene MacPike

Hop: K. T. Hoppin, "The Royal Society and Ireland"

HunA: Michael Hunter, *John Aubrey and the Realm of Learning*

HunR: Michael Hunter, *The Royal Society and Its Fellows, 1660-1700*

Hunt: Frederick Hunt, *Origins in Acoustics*

Huy.: *Oeuvres complètes de Christiaan Huygens*

Hyam: A. M. Hyamson, *Dictionary of Universal Biography*

IBNH: *Index bio-bibliographicus notorum hominum*

J: Christian Gottlieb Jöcher, *Allgemeines gelehrten Lexicon*

JB: Journal Book

LB: Letter Book

LBC: Letter Book Copy

LBO: Letter Book Original

LP: Letters and Papers

Munk: William Munk, *The Roll of the Royal College of Physicians of London*

NBU: *Nouvelle biographie universelle*

New.: *The Correspondence of Isaac Newton*, ed. H. W. Turnbull, et al.

NG: *New Grove Dictionary of Music and Musicians*

NUC: *National Union Catalogue*

Old.: *The Correspondence of Henry Oldenburg*, ed. A. Rupert and Marie Boas Hall

Pogg: J. Ch. Poggendorf, *Biographisch-literarisches Handwörterbuch*

PT: *Philosophical Transactions*

Ref.: Refer to (designates related, but not identical, articles in cross-references)

RB: Register Book

RBC: Register Book Copy

RBO: Register Book Original

R.S.: Royal Society

Sch: Percy Scholes, *Oxford Companion to Music*

Tay: E. G. R. Taylor, *Mathematical Practitioners of Tudor and Stuart England*

Trans.: Translation

Walis: Kazimierz Waliszewsky, *Paul the First of Russia*

PREFACE

The impetus for the present study arose from previous investigation by the authors into the role of music in the Paris Academy of Sciences during the seventeenth and eighteenth centuries. It seemed natural to direct a similar investigation to the other influential scientific body of the time where music also played a visible role, the Royal Society of London.

The Royal Society was founded earlier than the Paris Academy, in 1660; unlike its sister institution in France, whose functions were interrupted by the Revolution, it has enjoyed continuous activity to the present day. The current project begins with the founding of the Society and extends to 1806, the terminal date of the largest manuscript collection in the Society's archives (the *Letters and Papers),* which provides a convenient ending point for the present study.

Documents from the archives of the Royal Society help illuminate the changing view of music during this entire period. The emerging scientific empiricism of the seventeenth century, with its emphasis on experimentation and observation, is revealed through numerous descriptions of acoustical experiments in the Society's proceedings; at the same time, more practical areas of interest -- such as tuning systems, the therapeutic role of music in medicine, and the structure of musical instruments -- became viable for study by the encyclopedic scientist/philosophers of the day. However, this early concept of music as a valid field for scientific investigation was destined to give way to one in which acoustics within the science of physics was decidedly separated from music as an art. Indeed, during the second half of the eighteenth century, a steady decline of interest in music is increasingly evident, paralleling a similar decline in the Paris Academy at roughly the same time.

The major portion of this book is devoted to a bibliographical catalog of items on music found both in the Society's official publication, the *Philosophical Transactions*, and in nine manuscript collections residing in its archives. The introduction provides an interpretative study of these items, relating the work of the Society to that of other scientific bodies of the time. Both the catalog and the study should be of value not only to musicians but also to students of the history of science.

The catalog is divided into ten sections, corresponding to the ten document source collections of which it is comprised. Each collection is individually described, and within each section the bibliographical entries are organized chronologically. While dates cited in the entries are those that appear in the individual items being cataloged, the overall arrangement conforms to the English calendar in use at the time: the Julian calendar until September 2, 1752, and afterwards the Gregorian calendar. Most continental nations had abandoned the Julian calendar in favor of the Gregorian by the late sixteenth or early seventeenth centuries. Since the English did not, their dates lagged behind continental ones by ten days during the seventeenth century and eleven during the eighteenth.[1] In this catalog, manuscript documents dated in the Gregorian style prior to September 2, 1752 are provided with the equivalent Julian date in brackets.

Every item is accompanied by a short summary of its contents. For the printed documents, authors' names are spelled as they appear in the source,

---

[1] The discrepancy was caused by the fact that the Julian calendar failed to omit century years as leap years; it thus became increasingly inaccurate. The Gregorian calendar, still in use today, was adopted by the Catholic countries of Europe in 1582. England, however, did not change to the new calendar until the passage of the Calendar Act in 1752, which provided that the day after September 2 of that year was to be designated September 14. At the same time, the beginning of the year was moved back from March 25 (in the Julian system) to January 1 (Gregorian). Accordingly, prior to 1752, English documents dated January 1 through March 24 usually bear a double year designation (e.g., January 15, 1650/1), the earlier year indicating the "old style" (Julian) and the later the "new style" (Gregorian). Within this time frame, generally, care must be taken in the dating of documents designated by a single year.

while for the manuscripts, spellings are standardized. Titles are always spelled and punctuated as in the original document. In the citations, information in parenthesis is derived from the source; that in square brackets is provided by the present authors. Documents are in English unless otherwise noted.

Citations of book reviews are listed by author, title, and publication date of the book being reviewed, as well as by any additional title given to the review itself. The reviewer's name, if known, is cited in the descriptive summary (rather than as the author of the article). The designation "book review" is used to identify a critical study of the publication; "book notice" indicates either a simple listing, or a short, non-critical description.

Leta E. Miller
University of California, Santa Cruz

Albert Cohen
Stanford University

October 1986

ACKNOWLEDGMENTS

This project could not have materialized without the gracious cooperation of the library staff at the Royal Society; I should like particularly to thank N. H. Robinson, L. P. Townsend, S. M. Grover and A. G. Clark for their kind assistance. I am also very pleased to acknowledge the American Philosophical Society and the University of California Santa Cruz (UCSC) Committee on Research and Division of the Arts for granting funds to facilitate this work.

A number of scholars provided very helpful advice during the course of the research, among them Dr. Penelope Gouk and Profs. Neal Zaslaw, Sherwood Dudley, John Hajdu, Fredric Lieberman, Lionel Sawkins, and William Mahrt. Thanks are also due to the library staff at UCSC and to Mr. Jerry Persons at the Stanford University Music Library. A number of other libraries also provided very useful services, particularly the British Library and the UC Berkeley library system. The plates are reproduced by permission of the Royal Society.

L. E. M.

Music

in the

Royal Society of London

1660-1806

INTRODUCTION

That music formed an integral part of the study of science in earlier times has long been recognized. But it is only recently that the extent of its role in the scientific societies of Europe during the seventeenth and eighteenth centuries has come to light. Two societies then dominated the European scene: the Royal Society of London (founded in 1660 and formally incorporated in 1662) and the Académie Royale des Sciences in Paris (founded in 1666). The astonishing number and scope of musical concerns voiced by leading French scientists of the day, revealed in a recent study of the Paris Academy,[1] suggest that the relationship of music to science continued to be intense through much of the academic movement of the time. The present study of music in the Royal Society of London during the same period confirms the relationship.

The Royal Society was a rather different type of organization than the Académie Royale. Unlike the French body, the English society was supported philosophically, but not financially, by the Crown; in addition, its membership was not restricted in number. Without steady financial support from the government, the Royal Society periodically suffered from severe fiscal difficulties, and with no limitations on the number of members, the range of abilities of the scientists belonging to the Society was far more varied than in France. In short, the English body was less elitist and not as politically powerful

---

[1] Albert Cohen, *Music in the French Royal Academy of Sciences* (Princeton: Princeton University Press, 1981).

as the French; yet it could boast of members who were leaders in the world's scientific community -- members such as Isaac Newton, Robert Boyle, Robert Hooke, and Edmund Halley.

Music, clearly, was not the first concern of the Society. Nevertheless, a significant interest in various aspects of the subject is evident in the substantial body of material uncovered during recent archival study of sources dating from the organization's founding through its activities at the end of the eighteenth century. The results of this study form the basis for the present catalog, which is limited to the academy's printed journal and the manuscript documents that currently reside in the archives of the Royal Society Library.

The source collections from which documents were drawn are ten in number; each is treated in a separate section within the present catalog.

Printed source:
I. *The Philosophical Transactions* -- a series of volumes constituting the principal publication of the Society; founded in 1665 by the first secretary, Henry Oldenburg, the *Transactions* continue to be issued to the present day.

Manuscript sources:
II. *Early Letters* -- 38 volumes of original correspondence dating from 1660 to 1740.
III. *Classified Papers* -- original articles submitted to the Society between 1660 and 1740.
IV. *Letters and Papers* -- 120 volumes of both correspondence and articles dating from 1740 to 1806 (subsuming categories II and III).
V. *Letter Book* -- a series of volumes containing fair copies of a large part of the correspondence in the *Early Letters,* but also including some unique items.
VI. *Register Book* -- fair copies of many of the *Classified Papers,* including unique items as well.
VII. *Boyle Letters and Papers* -- a collection of correspondence

and papers by or belonging to Robert Boyle, one of the founding members of the Society.

VIII. *Extra manuscripts* -- five volumes of miscellaneous papers not included in the other series.

IX. *General manuscripts* -- a collection of miscellaneous manuscripts in the possession of the Society but not necessarily related to its proceedings.

X. *Journal Book* -- minutes of the Society's weekly meetings dating from its inception.

Among the items on music are significant documents on acoustics and theory, as well as writings by many of the foremost scientists and musicians of the time. Several of the authors cited herein wrote more extensively on music than is revealed in this catalog (e.g., Huygens and Newton); however, examination of documents found outside of the Society's publications or archives lies beyond the scope of the current project.[2]

Nevertheless, a broad picture is projected by the materials indexed here -- one that reflects the continuing interest of seventeenth- and eighteenth-century scientists in music and acoustics. These interests are grouped into seven categories, which are surveyed below.[3]

ACOUSTICS AND TEMPERAMENT

Many of the scientists active in the Society's early years were concerned with understanding the nature of sound itself, an interest reflected by numerous references to acoustical experiments in the *Journal Book* during the Society's first half century. In July and August of 1664, for example, experiments were

---

[2] For a study of music in the early years of the Royal Society (including documents both within and outside of the Royal Society archives), see Penelope Mary Gouk, "Music in the Natural Philosophy of the Early Royal Society" (Ph.D. diss., Warburg Institute, 1982).

[3] Volumes 1-70 of the *Philosophical Transactions* (source I), plus the index for these volumes, have been published in a reprint edition by Johnson Reprint Corp., Kraus Reprint Corp., New York, 1963. Microfilm copies of the achival manuscript sources listed in this catalog (derived from sources II through X) are on deposit at the Stanford University Music Library.

conducted on a vibrating brass wire, which was divided as a monochord; attempts were made to determine the frequency of vibration.[4] In July 1680, Robert Hooke showed the musical vibrations of a glass, and in the following year, he produced musical sounds with the teeth of a brass wheel.[5] Francis Hauksbee performed several experiments in 1704 and 1709 which proved that sound cannot be transmitted through a vacuum,[6] and in November 1715, John Theophilus Desaguilliers showed a manner of making the sound vibrations of a bell visible and audible "by means of a screw whose point the Bell struck against at every Dilatation made the same way."[7]

The *Journal Book* also records information on experiments conducted elsewhere. For example, in 1663, William Brouncker described the results of various tests made along the Thames, among which were observations on echoes and the velocity of sound.[8] The Society took considerable interest in Daniel George Morhof's tale of the breaking of a glass with a sonorous voice (1670),[9] and Francis Aston reported on a deaf man who could feel sound vibrations with his mouth well enough to tune an instrument (1715).[10] Robert Hooke (whose responsibilities as curator of the Society included providing experiments for the meetings) and Abraham Hill both described theories relating to the speed of sound (1689); and Robert Southwell and Edmund Halley are represented in discussions of sound transmission in water (1691).[11]

This is not to say that acoustics was the primary focus of attention either of the Society or of its individual members; in comparison to meteorology,

---

[4] For these and other experiments in 1664, see items X-12 through X-16.

[5] See items X-37 through X-39.

[6] Reviewed below, pp.12-13.

[7] Journal Book Copy, vol. 11, p. 85. See item X-73.

[8] See item VI-6.

[9] Published as *Epistola de scypho vitreo per certum humanae vocis sonum rupto. . . dissertatio* (Kiel, 1672). See items VIII-6 and X-25. Pepys also had some "singing glasses" made; see Robert Latham and William Matthews, eds., *The Diary of Samuel Pepys* (Berkeley and Los Angeles: University of California Press, 1970-83), vol. 9, p. 457 (Feb. 23, 1669).

[10] Journal Book, May 26, 1715. See item X-72.

[11] See items X-54 through X-56.

anatomy, or botany, for example, the number of items on acoustics is miniscule. Yet there was unquestionably a sustained interest in the subject during the early period.

This interest is reflected not only by references in the *Journal Book,* but also by published and manuscript papers in the Society's archives. Among the significant acoustical papers printed in the *Philosophical Transactions* is a well-known essay by the mathematician John Wallis (1677).[12] The author describes the discovery of nodes in strings, as revealed through experiments with sympathetic vibrations, and he adds the observation that if a string is struck at the node, the sound is unclear and "very confused . . . by reason that the point is disturbed which should be at rest."[13] It is not clear from his explanation whether Wallis understood the principle of the simultaneous vibration of a string in all of its modes.[14] Although he later acknowledged[15] that the phenomena described in this paper had actually been shown to him by Narcissus Marsh, and although William Noble and Thomas Pigot had previously demonstrated the existence of nodes,[16] Wallis' paper remains a significant contribution to the development of acoustical theory. One of the founding members of the Society, he maintained a lively interest in music until the end of his life, submitting letters and papers to the Society from 1664 until 1698 (when he was over 80 years old) on such topics as tuning systems, ancient music, and the speaking trumpet. In addition, he translated into Latin the works of several important Greek theorists, including Ptolemy, Porphyrus, and Bryennius.[17]

Unfortunately, Wallis was not always scrupulous in making proper attributions for the theories he cited. Besides the case of the *Philosophical*

---

[12] See item I-26.

[13] Ibid., p. 841. Robert Hooke also speaks of sympathetic vibrations in his "Curious Dissertation," item III-29 (reviewed below, p. 35).

[14] See Burdette Lamar Green, "The Harmonic Series from Mersenne to Rameau: An Historical Study of Circumstances Leading to Its Recognition and Application to Music" (Ph.D. diss., Ohio State University, 1969), p. 383; Wallis' work is discussed on pp. 380-83.

[15] In *De algebra tractatus* (1693). See ibid., p. 381.

[16] The discovery was made independently by the two men ca. 1673-74. See Gouk, "Music in the . . . Early Royal Society," p. 88.

[17] See items I-28 and I-45.

Transactions paper mentioned above, he was accused on several additional occasions of crediting himself with the experiments or discoveries of others. As John Aubrey remarks,

> Tis certaine that he is perhaps of reall worth, and may stand with much glory upon his owne basis, needing not to be beholding to any man for fame, of which he is so extremely greedy, that he steales flowers from others to adorne his owne cap -- e.g. he lies at watch, at Sir Christopher Wren's discourse, Mr. Robert Hooke's, Dr. William Holder, etc; putts downe their notions in his note booke, and then prints it, without owneing the authors.[18]

Dating even before Wallis' 1677 paper on sympathetic vibration are documents and letters in the Society's archives that deal with the nature of sound. Among these is a hitherto unknown *Tractatus Musicus* inserted in the "Extra Manuscripts" collection (see Plate 10).[19] The document, dated "Rome, August 6, 1665," is an incomplete copy, which appears to be in the hand of the Society's first secretary, Henry Oldenburg. (Oldenburg himself was in London at this time, however; the Society was not in session, having been recessed due to an epidemic of plague.) The primary emphasis of the treatise is on acoustics. Its thirteen chapters deal with the nature of sound; vibrating bodies including bells and strings; the relation of density, length, and tension of a string to pitch; the ear; harmonic ratios; and consonant and dissonant intervals. Various acoustical problems, as well as applications of mathematical theories, are presented by the author.[20]

---

[18] John Aubrey, *Brief Lives and Other Selected Writings,* ed. Anthony Powell (London: The Cresset Press, 1949), p. 155. The "Brief Lives" are taken from notebook entries compiled during the time Aubrey aided Anthony à Wood in the preparation of the *Athenae Oxoniensis* (published 1691-92). The "Lives" (which generally consist of anecdotes rather than biographies in the standard sense of the word) were never published in Aubrey's lifetime, although Wood drew extensively from the material. Excerpts from Aubrey's notes were printed in 1813 and first appeared *in toto* in Andrew Clark's edition of 1898. Another disputed article in the present catalog is Wallis' letter to Boyle regarding teaching speech to a deaf-mute (published in the *Transactions* of 1670; see item I-5). Wallis' claims were contested by William Holder, who describes his own teaching method in an appendix to his *Elements of Speech: An Essay of Inquiry into the Natural Production of Letters: With an Appendix concerning Persons Deaf and Dumb* (London: J. Martyn, 1669); see item IX-3 for a manuscript of the treatise. Holder's work, and Wallis' claims, are discussed by Aubrey in *Brief Lives,* p. 181. See also related items VIII-2 and X-2A.

[19] Item IX-2.

[20] Robert Hooke also discusses length and tension of a string in relation to pitch in his "Curious Dissertation," item III-29. See below, p. 35.

The *Transactions* of 1692 include a paper by Francis Robartes (or Roberts), in which the author questions why the 7th, 11th, 13th, and 14th harmonics on a trumpet are out of tune.[21] In this essay, which shows Robartes to be well aware of previous work on sympathetic vibrations and nodes in strings, he uses the trumpet-marine to illustrate the acoustical problems of the natural trumpet. After demonstrating that both instruments function acoustically in the same way, Robartes calculates string lengths for notes of the trumpet-marine and compares these lengths to those of the standard monochord tuning. He explains that the 7th, 11th, 13th, and 14th notes of the series do not coincide with pitches tuned in just intonation. Significantly, Robartes recognized that the harmonic series was infinite.[22]

Scientists in England, as on the continent, continued to seek a more accurate measurement for the speed of sound. Many of the Fellows, including Robert Boyle, Joshua Walker, and William Derham, attempted to determine the speed experimentally, while Isaac Newton calculated it theoretically. The work of Boyle and Newton is not detailed in documents in the Society's archives,[23] but that of Walker and Derham is. In an article which appeared in the *Transactions* of 1698,[24] Walker considered the impact of environmental factors on the speed of sound, concluding that the wind strongly affects its velocity. He also favored the theory that the speed of sound decreases as the wave propagates

---

[21] Item I-33.

[22] On Robartes' contributions to the development of acoustical theory, see Green, "The Harmonic Series," pp. 383-87.

[23] Although numerous references to Boyle's acoustical experiments may be found among the Society's documents, no details of his work are contained in the sources listed in the current index. His writing on the speed of sound is discussed by Gouk, "Music in the . . . Early Royal Society," p. 93. See *The Works of the Honourable Robert Boyle*, ed. Thomas Birch (London, 1744ff.; reprint, Hildesheim: Georg Olms, 1966), vol. 5, p. 7, for his measurement of over 400 yards per second. Newton calculated the speed of sound using analytic tools only. The calculations were published in the *Principia*, Book 2, sec. 8. His reasoning was accurate, but his measurement of 288 m/sec was low due to his failure to account for adiabatic heating of the air when it is compressed by sound waves. For a detailed discussion, see Sigalia Dostrovsky, "The Origins of Vibration Theory: The Scientific Revolution and the Nature of Music" (Ph.D. diss., Princeton University, 1969), pp. 215-36. See also Clifford A. Truesdell, "The Theory of Aerial Sound, 1687-1788" in *Leonhardi Euleri opera omnia*, ser. 2, vol. 13 (Lausanne: Societatis Scientiarum Naturalium Helveticae, 1955), pp. xxi-xxiv, and R. Bruce Lindsay, "The Story of Acoustics," in *Acoustics: Historical and Philosophical Development* (Stroudsburg, Pa.: Dowden, Hutchinson and Ross, 1972), pp. 5-20.

[24] See item I-43.

through the air.

Derham's experiments are described in a lengthy article published in the *Transactions* of 1708.[25] He reviews previous data from various scientists, and poses 19 questions about sound propagation which he attempted to answer by performing a series of tests. He addresses such questions as: the absolute speed of sound; the effect of temperature, air pressure, wind, weather, altitude, etc. on this speed; whether the direction in which a sound is propagated has an effect on its velocity; whether sounds of different timbres or volumes travel at the same speed; etc. Among the measurements for the velocity of sound cited by the author[26] are data by Flamsteed and Halley, although no report on the subject by these two scientists is found in the Society's proceedings.[27] Derham concludes (erroneously) that the only factor affecting the speed of sound is the wind.

Predating the articles by Walker and Derham are Lawrence Rooke's measurement of the velocity (mentioned in the minutes of 1668)[28] and Walter Charleton's discussion of experiments aimed at determining the correct speed of sound by the use of echoes (1662).[29] Earlier experiments had been performed elsewhere by Marin Mersenne, the Florentine Accademia del Cimento, and others.[30] However, since the effect of temperature was not then known (it was first recognized in the 1740s),[31] the data collected by these early scientists were conflicting.

The most reliable measurement for the speed of sound made in the eighteenth century resulted from experiments performed under the auspices of

---

[25] See item I-58.

[26] One of these is by Francis Robartes. See item I-35A.

[27] In item VI-19, however, Halley gives an approximate measurement of 300 mph for the speed of sound, which is quite different from the measurement attributed to him by Derham.

[28] See item X-18.

[29] See below, p. 15.

[30] The Accademia del Cimento existed from 1657 to 1667. For a detailed description of the academy and its members, see W. E. K. Middleton, *The Experimenters: A Study of the Accademia del Cimento* (London and Baltimore: Johns Hopkins Press, 1971).

[31] See Frederick Hunt, *Origins in Acoustics* (New Haven and London: Yale University Press, 1978), p. 110.

the Académie Royale des Sciences in Paris by Giovanni Domenico Maraldi and César-François Cassini de Thury in 1738.[32] Their work was cited ten years later in an article by William Watson, which compared the velocities of electricity and sound.[33] Watson reviewed the conflicting measurements of many earlier scientists and described experiments performed at Shooter's Hill on August 14, 1747, showing that electricity travelled much faster than sound.

Other documents in the Society's archives describe experiments on the media through which sound can be propagated. Especially noteworthy in this area is the work of Denis Papin in 1684-85 and Francis Hauksbee in 1705-09. Papin's work, by which he concluded that sound cannot travel through a vacuum, is described in three unpublished papers entered in the *Register Book*.[34] The first (read November 26, 1684) criticizes experiments conducted nearly twenty years earlier by the Accademia del Cimento and published in their *Saggi di naturali esperienze fatte nell' Accademia del Cimento* in 1667.[35] The Italian scientists, who tested the abilities of a bell and an organ pipe to produce sound while in a vacuum, concluded that it was indeed possible for sound to be propagated without air; however, their experimental equipment did not succeed in achieving a complete vacuum or in isolating the sounding agent from the container, and therefore their conclusions were unreliable.[36] Papin's second paper (read March 11, 1685) describes an improved version of one of the Florentine experiments -- the one using a pipe in a receiver -- and it resulted in his conclusion that no sound could be produced when the air was exhausted (see Plate 8).[37] The final paper (read the following week) describes a more complex

---

[32] Their work was published in the *Histoire* and the *Mémoires* of the Paris Academy. See Albert Cohen and Leta E. Miller, *Music in the Paris Academy of Sciences, 1666-1793*, Detroit Studies in Music Bibliography, 43 (Detroit: Information Coordinators, 1979), pp. 32-33, nos. I-58 and I-61.

[33] Item I-76.

[34] Items VI-12 through VI-14.

[35] This is the academy's only publication; no individual authors are cited, but the experiments are described in some detail. For a commentary and English translation, see Middleton, *The Experimenters*.

[36] For a description of the experiment, see Middleton, *The Experimenters*, pp. 151-54.

[37] Boyle had proposed this test in his *New Experiments Physico-Mechanical* (see *Boyle Works*, vol. 1, p. 64; other acoustical experiments are also described therein and in document IX-1). The

version of the previous experiment, but presents no conclusions.

The experiments conducted by Papin and the Florentines were by no means new. The one with a bell in a vacuum had been tried by Gianfrancesco Sagredo as early as 1615, and similar work was described by Athanasius Kircher (1650) and Otto von Guericke (1672).[38] In 1660, Robert Boyle had published the results of equivalent tests using both a watch and a bell in a receiver, creating a near vacuum with his improved air pump; he had drawn conclusions quite opposite to those of the Accademia del Cimento.[39] Later experiments by Boyle similarly disproved the Italian theories.[40] However, in 1684 the issue was revived by the publication of Richard Waller's English translation of the *Saggi;* it was this book, reviewed in the *Transactions* of the same year,[41] that apparently stimulated Papin's work.

Further tests of this type were carried out by Francis Hauksbee in the early eighteenth century. On several occasions in 1704, 1705, and 1709,[42] Hauksbee either performed experiments on sound at the Society's meetings or read papers describing experiments he had completed elsewhere. The results of these tests were published in a series of short papers in the *Transactions* (March 1705 and May-June 1709).[43] Hauksbee repeated and refined the old experiment of the bell in the vacuum and showed once again that the sound decreased in

---

experiment consisted of inserting a bellows and a musical pipe into a container in such a way that the bellows could be operated from the outside after the air in the container had been pumped out. For the Florentine experiment, see Middleton, *The Experimenters*, pp. 152-54. Papin's experiment omitted the bellows entirely; the pipe was attached directly to the the the stopper, which then functioned in place of the bellows.

[38] See Hunt, *Origins in Acoustics*, pp. 112-18. Guericke's work is found in *Experimenta nova (ut vocantur) Magdeburgia di vacuo spatio* (Amsterdam, 1672); Kircher's in *Musurgia universalis* (Rome, 1650).

[39] See his *New Experiments Physico-Mechanical, Touching the Spring of the Air, and its Effects* (1660), in *Boyle Works*, vol. 1, pp. 62ff.

[40] In his *Continuation of New Experiments Physico-Mechanical*. See *Boyle Works*, vol. 3, pp. 259ff.

[41] See item I-31.

[42] March 8 and 15, 1704 (see items X-63 and X-64); May 16 and June 13, 1705 (Journal Book mentions that an experiment was performed or a paper read, but without any description); and June 1, 8, 15, and 29, and November 2, 1709 (see III-24, 25, and 26, and X-66).

[43] Items I-51, I-52, and I-60 through I-62.

intensity as the air was withdrawn. He also demonstrated several modifications of the experiment, such as increasing the air in the receiver and placing the bell in a double receiver, the inner one filled with air and the outer one containing a vacuum. Like Papin, Boyle, and others, he concluded that air was indeed necessary for sound. In a separate experiment, Hauksbee also confirmed that sound could be transmitted through water.[44]

Three other significant acoustical papers appeared in the *Transactions* during the same period as Hauksbee's work. These include the article by William Derham cited above (1708), Guido Grandi's paper on the shape and the paths of sound waves emitted from a vibrating body in a non-uniform medium (1709),[45] and Brook Taylor's important work on the motion of a vibrating string (1713).[46] The last work, in particular, marked an important step in the understanding of acoustics. A mathematician and amateur musician, Taylor succeeded in deriving from the fundamental principles of dynamics a theory governing the vibration of a string in the fundamental mode. The author first shows that the curvature of a string at a particular point is proportional to the distance of that point from the axis. In a second lemma, he proves that the transverse force (or the acceleration) on a given part of the string is proportional to the curvature. Using these two principles, Taylor demonstrates that if a string is stretched and released, all points will reach the original unstretched position at the same time, thus proving that the frequency of vibration is independent of the amplitude. With this information, Taylor was able to derive the exact frequency of vibration in the fundamental mode for a string of a given length.

In addition to these major articles, numerous shorter references to acoustics occur in notations in the *Journal Book* and in letters to the Society. Among the latter, one should note those of Christiaan Huygens (on the division of the monochord, experiments on sound propagation, etc.; see Plate 7) and of

---

[44] See item I-62.

[45] See item I-59.

[46] Item I-63.

Ignace-Gaston Pardies (observations on experiments regarding sound).[47] Intense interest is expressed by Oldenburg and many of his correspondents in Pietro Mengoli's treatise on music (published in 1670)[48] and in acoustical experiments performed by other scientific bodies. Comparisons between sound and light are also frequent, not only in the works of Isaac Newton,[49] but also in a lengthy paper by the Irish bishop Narcissus Marsh (which was presented to the Dublin Society in 1683 and later printed in the *Transactions*),[50] in papers by Robert Hooke,[51] and in Thomas Young's Bakerian lecture "On the Theory of Light and Colours" read in 1801.[52]

Acoustical studies dealing with the nature of echoes and the description and physical cause of "whispering places" were particularly numerous in the early years of the Society. In fact, four papers on these subjects were written in 1661-62. The earliest, by Robert Southwell, concerns several whispering places and locations with multiple echoes; the paper was not presented to the Society until nearly a century later, however, when Henry Miles communicated it to the membership, and it was subsequently published in the *Transactions* of 1746. Southwell describes two whispering places, one in Italy and one in France, but emphasizes that neither is as good as the one in Gloucester Abbey in England.[53] He also relates experiments with echoes, one in Brussels which reverberated 15 times, and one near Milan which was heard to repeat 56 times.

The other three essays are filed in the *Classified Papers* and copied into

---

[47] See, for example, items II-1, II-2, II-6, and II-24.

[48] *Speculationi di musica* (Bologna, 1670).

[49] See items I-14, I-19, and VI-11.

[50] See item I-30

[51] See, for example, item VI-9. Other references may be found in *The Posthumous Works of Robert Hooke,* ed. Richard Waller (1705; reprint, ed. T. M. Brown, London: Frank Cass & Co., 1971), pp. 116 and 134. According to Waller, these presentations were made to the Society ca. May 1681 and April or May 1682.

[52] Published in 1802. See item I-127.

[53] Francis Bacon had described the whispering place in Gloucester in the *Sylva sylvarum.* See Gouk, "Music in the . . . Early Royal Society," pp. 29-30 and note 15. John Evelyn also describes the phenomenon in his diary (July 31, 1654), and it was the subject of a paper presented to the Society by Henry Powle (item III-6).

the *Register Book.*[54] The earliest of the three (read September 10, 1662), was written by the physician Walter Charleton and relates experiments on the velocity of sound as tested by echoes.[55] The author reviews conflicting opinions by Mersenne and Kircher on echoes and the speed of sound, presenting his own observations as well. Charleton questions Mersenne's theory that all sounds move at the same speed, and proposes experiments to test the velocity of direct sounds at various volumes and with differing timbres, the velocity of reflected sounds, and the effect of the reflecting distance on the clarity of echoes of various lengths.[56]

The second paper, that of Henry Powle (October 29, 1662), describes the famous whispering place in the Gloucester Abbey, a narrow curved passage in which "every soft and gentle whisper [is] . . . as distinctly heard the whole length of the passage, as if you had applied your ear close to the mouth of the speaker."[57] Powle speculates that the cause of this effect is "the closeness of the passage, the voice being carried here, as in a hollow pipe or trunk."[58] Like many other seventeenth century scientists, he compares the propagation of sound to the circular waves produced by a stone being thrown into a pool of water. A figure of the same whispering place, attributed to John Aubrey, appears in a different volume of the *Classified Papers* (see Plate 4).[59]

The last of the papers mentioned above was authored by Robert Moray, one of the Society's founders and its president for one year (1660-61) before the organization's formal incorporation. Moray's work (dated December 3, 1662) describes an experiment in which a trumpet tune played at a Bay near Glasgow was followed by three distinct echoes. The author not only presents a map of the

---

[54] Two of them (those by Henry Powle and Robert Moray) were printed *in toto* by Thomas Birch in his *History of the Royal Society.* See items X-3 and X-6.

[55] See item III-5

[56] Charleton's theories of sound are discussed more fully in his *Physiologia Epicuro-Gassendo-Charltoniana* (1654). See Gouk, "Music in the . . . Early Royal Society," pp. 39ff., for a detailed description of them.

[57] Item X-3, p. 121.

[58] Ibid., p. 122

[59] See item III-7. Aubrey's name has been written in pencil in the index to the *Classified Papers.* It is possible that the drawing was made by William Wynde, however. See III-7 for

bay, but also notates the tune which was played.[60]

After Taylor's 1713 article on vibrating strings, little of significance concerning acoustics appears in the *Transactions* for much of the eighteenth century. However, one must not overlook Watson's article comparing the speed of sound and electricity (cited above), and the lengthy paper on "Experiments and Inquiries Respecting Sound and Light" by Thomas Young, which was published in 1800.[61] In this comprehensive study, Young presents the results of a variety of experiments on sound, including

> the measurement of the quantity of air discharged through an aperture; the determination of the direction and velocity of a stream of air proceeding from an orifice; ocular evidence of the nature of sound; the velocity of sound; sonorous cavities; the degree of divergence of sound; the decay of sound; the harmonic sounds of pipes; the vibrations of different elastic fluids; the analogy between light and sound; the coalescence of musical sounds; the frequency of vibrations constituting a given note; the vibrations of chords; the vibrations of rods and plates; the human voice; the temperament of musical intervals.[62]

Young's work strongly confirmed the wave nature of light and sound through his establishment of the principle of interference in 1802.[63]

Related to the question of acoustics is, of course, the problem of tuning systems. Among the discussions of this issue in the early years are those by Wallis (1664 and 1698), who presents results of mathematical calculations of intervals (although he advocates equal temperament on keyboard instruments), Christiaan Huygens (1661 and 1664), who briefly describes certain tuning problems, and John Birchensha (1661ff.), who presents his own mathematical division of the octave.[64] On the other hand, in 1664, Birchensha was asked to observe an experiment comparing a monochord tuned mathematically with one tuned by ear, and "he could not by his ear distinguish any difference in sounds

---

discussion.

[60] See item III-9.

[61] Item I-121.

[62] *Philosophical Transactions*, 1800, part 1, pp. 106-07.

[63] See Hunt, *Origins in Acoustics*, p. 132.

[64] For Wallis, see items II-3, II-4, II-5, I-39, and I-40; for Huygens, II-1 and II-6. Birchensha's work is described below, under section 5.

(upon the moving of the bridge) above half an inch, especially in the fourths, thirds and tones."[65]

In a letter from Florence dated 1672, Thomas Platt includes a digression on Pietro Salvetti's tuning of the lira viol "so as to make it wholly perfect." Salvetti, "one of the G. Duke's Musitians," invented a tuning such that "you may express upon [the instrument] all Concords, Discords, and also the imperfect Concords, as seavenths, sixths, etc. as well as upon any Virginal that hath the quarters of notes upon it."[66]

In 1705, a similar invention was shown to the Society by Thomas Salmon, who presented a viol fingerboard with altered placement of the frets so as to create mathematically accurate intervals. Salmon had been working with new tuning and temperament systems for many years, beginning with his suggestions for tuning changes in viols and lutes in the *Essay to the Advancement of Musick* (1672), and his proposal for a series of mathematically tuned fingerboards corresponding to various keys in his *Proposal to Perform Musick in Perfect and Mathematical Proportions* (1688). His demonstration at the meeting of June 27, 1705 is described in an article published in the *Transactions* in August of that year;[67] included is a plate showing a fingerboard appropriate to C major and A minor, with the frets placed so as to create perfect fifths and fourths (3:2 and 4:3) and "greater" and "lesser" thirds. The greater third is divided into a major tone (9:8) and a minor tone (10:9), and each of these is unequally divided, creating four sizes of semitones (17:16, 18:17, 19:18, and 20:19). In addition, the distance between E-F and B-C created a fifth "hemitone," 16:15. On July 3 the Fellows heard a performance of a Corelli sonata using this new fingerboard; the performers were Frederick and Christian Steffkin and "Gasperini" (i.e., Gasparo Visconti).[68] Later discussions of tuning may be found in letters and

---

[65] See Birch, *History of the Royal Society*, p. 458 (item X-13).

[66] *Philosophical Transactions*, vol. 7, no. 87, p. 5064. See item I-13.

[67] See item I-56; cf. X-65.

[68] See items I-56 and X-65. The Steffkin brothers were the sons of the German viol player and composer, Theodore Steffkin (d. 1673), who emigrated to England before 1634. Frederick and Christian were royal musicians. Gasperini refers to Gasparo Visconti (1683-1713), Italian violinist and composer; he should not be confused with Francesco Gasparini. (See *New Grove*, s.v. "Visconti.") Other musical performances for the Fellows are noted by Evelyn and Pepys in their

papers by Jean-Philippe Rameau (1750), Tiberius Cavallo (1788), and Thomas Young (1800).

MUSICAL INSTRUMENTS AND OTHER INVENTIONS

Unlike the activity of the Paris academy, that of the Royal Society showed little evidence of the revolutionary developments in instrument building that took place during the eighteenth century.[69] Not that English inventions were lacking in this regard; indeed, Bennet Woodcroft presents abridged descriptions of 55 patents for musical inventions from 1694 through 1800.[70] These include important (and not-so-important) improvements to string, wind, and keyboard instruments, new varieties of musical typography, newly invented instruments, a metronome, and even two automatic page turners. The Society, itself, however, took hardly any notice of these inventions. The only references to new instruments occur in a letter of 1684 by John Davis which mentions a manner of "contriving" several sorts of instruments so that any tune may be played on them, communications about a new mechanical instrument invented by Dom Robert Desgabetz (1669) and a new organ invented by "M. Perrot" (= Claude Perrault, 1685), Oldenburg's mention of a performance on the "archiviole" (1664), and a presentation by "Mr. Long" of an instrument which combined the harp and spinet (1712).[71]

Desgabetz' instrument contained strings spanning a two-octave range, which were sounded by a rotating drum operated by hand, by foot, or by an

---

diaries, but are not recorded in the minutes; see E. S. de Beer, ed., *Diary of John Evelyn* (Oxford: Clarendon Press, 1955), vol. 3, p. 377, and Pepys, *Diary*, vol. 5, p. 238. These performances apparently took place after the meetings on August 3 and 10, 1664 and featured Birchensha.

[69] The Paris academy took a leading role in approving inventions, among which were musical instruments. See Cohen, *Music in the French Royal Academy*, ch. 3.

[70] A listing of these patents is found in Bennet Woodcroft, *Subject-Matter Index of Patents of Invention, from March 2, 1617 . . . to October 1, 1852* (London, George Edward Eyre and William Spottiswoode, 1857). Summaries of all of the patents may be found in *Patents for Inventions*, vol. 26 (London, 1871).

[71] For Davis, see item V-14; for Desgabetz, item II-16. Perrault's organ is mentioned in a letter from Henri Justel (see V-17). For the Oldenburg reference, see item II-8. Mr. Long may refer to Roger Long; the instrument is described in the *Journal Book* (see X-69).

assistant. Depressing a key caused a string to be lifted into contact with the drum. The author extols the advantages of the instrument over the theorbo, harp, and viol, particularly emphasizing its capability of producing a larger volume of sound. His letter was read to the Society on December 2, 1669, but the value of his invention was seriously questioned.[72]

The Oldenburg reference is especially intriguing because it describes a musical performance at a meeting which is not recorded in the minutes.[73] In a letter to Robert Boyle, dated October 13, 1664, Oldenburg comments:

> Part of our yesterday's Entertainment at Gresham was ye hearing of some concerts upon a revived musicall instrument, called Archiviole, invented by a Frenchman 21. years ago . . . comprehending both an organ and a concert of 5. or 6. viols in one, giving an excellent harmony, very solemne and most fit for religious musick; but only yt ye multitude of strings maketh it somewhat longsom and tedious to tune . . . . I must confesse, it transports me . . . .[74]

Pepys and Evelyn both report hearing the instrument on October 5.[75] Pepys, in particular, was much more critical than was Oldenburg:

> The new instrument was brought, called the Arched Viall - where, being tuned with Lutestrings and played on with Kees like an Organ - a piece of Parchment is alway kept moving; and the strings, which by the keys are pressed down upon it, are grated, in imitation of a bow, by the parchment; and so it is intended to resemble several vyalls played on with one bow - but so basely and harshly, that it will never do . . . . After three hours' stay, it could

---

[72] See item X-23.

[73] Thomas Birch adds a footnote to the minutes of October 12, 1664, citing Oldenburg's letter. See item X-16.

[74] *The Correspondence of Henry Oldenburg*, ed. A. Rupert and Marie Boas Hall (Madison: University of Wisconsin Press, 1965-77), vol. 2, pp. 251-52. See item II-8. The "Entertainment at Gresham" refers to the Society's early meeting place at Gresham College. Praetorius describes a similar instrument, called the "Geigenwerk, Geigeninstrument, Geigenclavicymbel; or Violin-Clavier," invented by a Hans Hayden. See Michael Praetorius, *Syntagma musicum*, vol. 2, *De organographia*, section XLIV and plate III (translation by Harold Blumenfeld, New York: Bärenreiter, 1962, p. 67). See also Albert Cohen, "A Study of Instrumental Practice in Seventeenth-Century France," *Galpin Society Journal* 15 (1962): 10.

[75] Pepys says it was at a "musique-meeting" at the post office. Evelyn says it was at the Society, which conflicts with Oldenburg's reported date. See Pepys, *Diary*, vol. 5, p. 290, and Evelyn, *Diary*, vol. 3, p. 378.

not be Fixt in tune . . . .[76]

The idea did not die easily, however. The Paris Academy reviewed several similar instruments, including one by Jean LeVoir presented in 1742, which looked like a harpsichord, but sounded like a group of stringed instruments.[77]

Long's instrument is described in the minutes for June 12, 1712 thus: "The harp . . . [was] fixed on the top of the spinett which was so ordered that upon touching any of the keys one sett of jacks struck the string of the spinett and another sett those of the harp . . . ."[78] Each instrument could also be played separately. The bass strings of the spinet were made of metal, but the upper ones were of catgut, so as to better blend with the gut strings of the harp. A foot pedal regulated the jacks, making the plucking action stronger or weaker, thus controlling volume changes. No such instrument is known to have been patented by Mr. Long in England during the eighteenth century, however.[79]

As for musical inventions other than instruments, an article by John Freke, published in the *Transactions* of 1747, describes a machine invented by a Reverend Creed which could notate improvised compositions as they were played on the keyboard (see Plate 1).[80] The device featured a scroll of paper mounted behind the keys, and pencils attached to the keys themselves. As a note was played, the pencil made a mark of varying length (indicating duration) and height (indicating pitch) on the paper. The minutes record a discussion of this invention with some debate about whether, in fact, the device would work.[81] Other references to musical inventions in archival documents include a communication from Vincenzo Viviani in Italy on the use of pendulums as

---

[76] Pepys, *Diary*, vol. 5, p. 290. Evelyn reports that the instrument was shaped like a harpsichord.

[77] See Cohen, *Music in the French Royal Academy*, p. 54 and Plate 10. See also, Cohen and Miller, *Music in the Paris Academy of Sciences*, p. 59, no. III-13.

[78] Item X-69, p. 408.

[79] In 1788, a Parisian maker named Lami submitted a similar instrument to the Académie Royale des Sciences. Lami's invention was a combined forte-piano and harp (see Cohen and Miller, *Music in the Paris Academy of Sciences*, p. 69, and Cohen, *Music in the French Royal Academy*, p. 64). Several other such *instruments organisés* were presented to the French academy in the eighteenth century (see Cohen, ibid., ch. 3).

[80] Item I-74.

[81] See item X-87.

musical time-keepers and a report on a mechanical flute player invented by the Frenchman Jacques de Vaucanson, which was being shown in London in 1742.[82]

While eschewing interest in traditional musical instruments, the Society did show considerable concern for the development of an otacousticon (or "ear trumpet"), a device designed to magnify sound for the hard-of-hearing, as well as a "speaking trumpet," used to amplify the voice. In April 1668, Robert Hooke demonstrated ear trumpets made of glass and tin,[83] and later that year John Beale told Oldenburg of a Mr. Watkins of Oxford who had an otacousticon "by wch he could heare Sermons, Lectures, & Disputations very Well, even when he sate in some Corner, or at remoter distance than ye Croud, wch could heardly heare it."[84] Oldenburg apparently asked John Wallis about Beale's report (the letter is not extant), for Wallis replied that he had seen the device 14 or 16 years previously:

> To us who needed it not, I do not remember that it gave any considerable advantage . . . otherwise than that it did make ye noise seem greater; but, withall, more confused & indistinct. But it's possible yt if wee had been habitually accustomed to it, as he by use had been, it might as well have been advantageous to us allso.[85]

Wallis' letter includes a rough sketch of the instrument.

Interest in the topic of speaking trumpets was stimulated by the publication of Samuel Morland's *Tuba stentoro-phonica* in 1671. The work was favorably reviewed in the *Transactions* of January 1672, where it is stated that the largest trumpet (5 feet 6 inches, with a 21-inch diameter at the wide end and a 2-inch diameter at the small end) was able to project sounds for two to three

---

[82] An English edition by J. T. Desagulliers of Vaucanson's treatise describing this invention was published in London in the same year: *An Account of the Mechanism of an Automaton* (London: T. Parker, 1742). See item X-82 and Cohen, *Music in the French Royal Academy*, p. 67.

[83] Item X-20. Pepys claims that the glass otacousticon was merely a broken bottle, but that it was effective. See Pepys, *Diary*, vol. 9, p. 146.

[84] The letter is dated August 29, 1668; see *Correspondence of Henry Oldenburg*, no. 951. The original document is not in the Royal Society library, but in the British Library, Sloane 4294, ff. 26-27.

[85] *Correspondence of Henry Oldenburg*, no. 954, vol. 5, p. 34 (see item II-14).

miles.[86]

Oldenburg spread the news of Morland's invention throughout Europe, extolling it to his correspondents in France, Italy, and elsewhere.[87] The new invention also excited discussion and controversy at the Académie Royale des Sciences in France;[88] in February 1672 Francis Vernon wrote to Oldenburg from Paris that

> they have made a trumpett here as neare as they can to the measures and description of Sr. Samuel Moreland and it hath succeeded very well and beene heard at the distance of 4000 Toyses [i.e., fathoms].[89]

By April of that year, Vernon was able to report that the French trumpet he described in February had been compared to one of Morland's own instruments and performed just as well.[90] In addition, Christopher Kirkby wrote to Oldenburg about a device made in Dantzig following the description in the *Transactions*, which was "not without success."[91]

Another report from France came from Ignace-Gaston Pardies, who discussed at length the advantage of giving a hyperbolic shape to the instrument.[92] On the other hand, Morland's priority of invention was challenged by Athanasius Kircher, who claimed to have invented a similar device 24 years earlier which could carry sound from three to four miles.[93]

In June 1672, the Fellows heard descriptions and witnessed tests of

---

[86] See item I-9.

[87] See items II-23, II-28, II-29, and II-33, for example.

[88] See Hunt, *Origins in Acoustics*, pp. 125-27.

[89] Item II-32. The trumpet was made by Jean Denis. See *Correspondence of Henry Oldenburg*, no. 1914.

[90] Item II-34.

[91] See item II-40.

[92] Item II-35. The theory was first presented by N. Cassegrain. See Hunt, *Origins in Acoustics*, p. 127.

[93] See items II-36 and II-37.

speaking trumpets by Hooke, John Conyers, and Jonathan Goddard,[94] and in 1675 Newton sent Oldenburg a figure and description of Thomas Mace's ear trumpet, as given to him by Mace's son.[95] Conyers later developed an improved (shorter) model of Morland's instrument which is described in an article in the *Transactions* of 1678,[96] and as late as 1699 Robert Hooke still showed interest in such devices when he reviewed Jean de Hautefeuille's work in this area.[97] Manuscript catalogs of the Society's museum list several varieties of such acoustical devices.[98]

Other references to instruments in the Society's proceedings concern various types of drums. A "magical drum" from Lapland was donated to the Society by a "Swedish gentleman," Mr. Heisig, in 1681.[99] Along with the instrument was a "beater or drum-hammer" and "a piece of brass with rings hanging by chains," which was placed on the drum and made to bounce as the instrument was struck.

Another Lapland drum is described in an anonymous letter entered in the *Register Book* ca. 1702-06.[100] The author describes a ceremony in which the drum, carved from a tree and decorated with "characters," was beaten continuously until the musician went into a trance. According to the article, the wooden instrument was similar to the type used by American Indians in rain ceremonies.

Still another drum, a Siamese instrument donated by John Short, is described by Nehemiah Grew in his *Musaeum Regalis Societatis or a Catalogue and Description of the Natural and Artificial Rarities Belonging to the Royal*

---

[94] Items X-30 and X-31

[95] See II-43 and H. W. Turnbull, et al., *The Correspondence of Isaac Newton* (Cambridge: Cambridge University Press, 1959-77), no. 144. Mace's otacousticon was 2 feet long and 8 inches in diameter at the wide end.

[96] Item I-27

[97] See III-16.

[98] See below, pp. 25-26 for discussion of musical items in the museum.

[99] See item X-40. The drum is listed in several manuscript catalogs of the Society's museum. See item VI-21 for details.

[100] See item VI-21. Although undated, the letter can be placed in this time period by comparison with the surrounding entries.

Society and Preserved at Gresham Colledge [sic] (London, 1681). This instrument consisted of a varnished earthen jug covered with a stretched fish-skin.[101]

In 1774, the explorer Tobias Furneaux[102] donated instruments to the Society that he had acquired on a visit to Tongatabu, the largest island of Tonga (then known as the Isle of Amsterdam).[103] The instruments were given to the Irish writer Joshua Steele, who reported on them in two papers read to the Society in January and February 1775 and published in the *Transactions* for that year. Steele describes two sets of pipes -- a smaller one with nine pipes, and a larger one with ten -- as well as a nose flute from Tahiti (see Plate 2). For each of the pipes, he details the possible pitches, including its lowest-sounding tone and all notes obtainable by overblowing. For five of the nine pipes of the smaller set, he was able to overblow at a fifth, an octave, and a major tenth. For the others, however, he was only able to produce a fifth and a minor tenth, a phenomenon for which he had no explanation. (A similar situation held true for the larger pipe set.) The nose-flute was capable of producing only four pitches plus out-of-tune octaves, but Steele shows that an interesting variety of tunes can be played on the instrument, and he even presents a series of such pieces.

Other articles deal with instruments discovered in archeological searches. For example, in a letter of December 29, 1712,[104] Francis Nevill described brass trumpets found in Ireland several years previously. The minutes of January 29, 1713 record two letters being read on the subject, the first dated December 17, 1699, from Edward Lhuyd, keeper of the Ashmolean museum, giving "an account of a Copper Trumpet with the hole for sounding in the midst," and the letter by Nevill written 13 years later in which "was a sketch of the Trumpets

---

[101] Grew, p. 368.

[102] Tobias Furneaux (1735-81) was the first explorer to circumnavigate the globe in both directions. He traveled to the South Seas in 1773 and returned to England in July 1774. See *Encyclopedia Britannica*.

[103] See items I-101, 102, and 103, and related articles. Tongatabu was discovered by the Dutch explorer Abel Tasman, and named Amsterdam on January 19, 1643. See *Pacific Islands*, vol. 1 (British Naval Intelligence Division, 1945), p. 251.

[104] Published in the *Transactions* in 1713. See item I-64.

before mentioned."[105] According to Nevill, a total of eight instruments were discovered. He provides a description and figures for two of them, which show trumpets with a bent configuration, a conical bore, and a mouth hole on the side. He also discusses a gold instrument having two bell-like objects joined by a curved handle, but cannot provide an explanation of its use. In 1761, Richard Pococke, Bishop of Ossory, described similar instruments -- specifically, brass trumpets, presumed to be Danish, found in a bog in the County of Cork in Ireland; one of these had its embouchure hole on the side.[106]

In an article published in the *Transactions* in 1702, the Irish physician Thomas Molyneux concluded from a passage in Horace that the ancient lyre was made from a tortoise shell. Molyneux draws support for his conclusion from other writers and even presents a diagram of the instrument. A later article by George Pearson (published in 1796) contains information on the metallurgical content of a *lituus,* an ancient Roman trumpet which (along with other ancient implements) was discovered in Lincolnshire when the bed of the river Witham was scoured in 1787-88. Unfortunately, Pearson melted down the instrument before subjecting its metal to a number of scientific tests.[107]

In its first century of existence, the Society maintained a museum containing curious and unusual objects, as well as some new inventions. The contents of this repository were donated to the British Museum in 1781, when the Society moved to new quarters at Somerset House. However, records of the collection are found in several sources, including Grew's *Musaeum Regalis Societatis . . .* and five manuscript catalogs.[108] The musical or acoustical devices mentioned are as follows:

> Three otacousticons, one of ivory, one of copper, and one of tin; according to Grew, the ivory one, donated by Wilkins, is best (Grew; Mss. 413, 417).

---

[105] *Journal Book Copy,* vol. 10, pp. 447-48. See item X-70.

[106] See item IV-22.

[107] See item I-116

[108] Royal Society mss. no. 413-417.

"An Acoustic Trochlea of a circular Figure," another "of a cylindric figure," a third "with a strait tube" (Ms. 417).

The Siamese drum donated by John Short (Grew; Mss. 414, 416).

The Lapland drum donated by Heisig (Mss. 414, 416).

An Indian drum (Ms. 417).

"Castanets made of ye Husk of Siliquose plant given by Mr. Doody. Feb. 5, 1695/6" (Ms. 414).

"Castinets made of the Husks of Indian Beans" (Ms. 417).

An African guitar, an ivory flute, a Chinese organ (Ms. 414).

"A pair of Organs from fort St. George" donated by Mr. Buckley on April 22, 1702 (Ms. 416).

"A Chinese musical Instrument, about six feet long, composed of unequal Tubes" (Ms. 417).

ANATOMY: THE EAR AND THE VOICE

The Society heard numerous papers on anatomy, including studies on the structure of the ear and on the human voice, to both of which musical production and perception are obviously linked. An article by William Holder which appeared in the Transactions in 1668, for example,[109] contains speculations on the functions of various parts of the ear. Holder maintains that the purpose of the ear drum is merely protective, keeping dirt and dust away from the auditory nerve. This, he claims, is proven by experiments on a dog, which showed that the animal could hear even after the ear drum was broken.[110] Nevertheless, Holder hypothesized that if the ear drum is not taut it will interfere with the accurate reception of sound. He thus devised an experiment to help a man who was nearly deaf; by beating very loudly on a drum held close to the man's ear, Holder claimed to create a wind which stretched the membrane tightly. He asserted that while the drum was beating, the man could hear words

---

[109] See item I-3

[110] A similar discussion took place at a meeting on March 8, 1699. See item X-58.

spoken softly near him, but could not hear much louder sounds when the drum-beating stopped.[111]

Fifteen years later, a review of Joseph-Guichard Du Verney's important *Traité de l'organe de l'ouie* was published in the *Transactions*.[112] The reviewer provides a detailed summary of Du Verney's book, which had received the strong endorsement of the Académie Royale des Sciences.[113] Although incorrect in some of his conclusions about the function of various parts of the ear,[114] Du Verney provided anatomical descriptions which were largely correct and his treatise marked a significant step in the development of an accurate picture of the ear's function.[115]

In the same year as the Du Verney review, William Musgrave wrote Francis Aston from Oxford about a Dr. Aldrege who hypothesized that there must be two ear drums "for the Causeing Harmony,"[116] and Edme Mariotte wrote Aston about his own hypothesis on the perception of sound:

> Mon hypothèse est que le sentiment de tous les sons réside dans la membrane intérieure qui envelope les nerfs . . . . Par cette hypothèse j'ay jugé, quil n'y devoit avoir aucune branche du nerf Auditif . . . mais seulement une extension et distribution de la membrane qui les envelope intérieurement . . . .[117]

---

[111] Holder gives details on teaching speech to a deaf-mute in his *Elements of Speech*. See above, footnote 18.

[112] The review appeared in the same year as the book was published, 1683. See item I-29.

[113] Beginning in 1677, Du Verney had presented many of his findings on the ear to the Paris academy and that body had strongly supported his treatise. See Cohen, *Music in the French Royal Academy*, pp. 10-11.

[114] For example, he placed the principal organ of hearing in the semi-circular canals and vestibule as well as in the cochlea. He hypothesized that the sound receptor of the inner ear was the bony spiral lamina and he erroneously assumed that the inner ear was filled with air. Du Verney also felt that the folds in the outer ear helped magnify sounds. See Ernest Glen Wever and Merle Lawrence, *Physiological Acoustics* (Princeton: Princeton University Press, 1954), pp. 6-9.

[115] Du Verney was the first to provide a figure of the basilar membrane, for example. See Ernest Glen Wever, *The Theory of Hearing* (New York: John Wiley and Sons, 1949), p. 13.

[116] See item V-10, p. 54. Mengoli had described two ear drums in his *Musica speculativa* (1670); see review in the *Transactions*, item I-21. The review also discusses Mengoli's views on the properties of sound.

[117] "My hypothesis is that the sensation of all sound resides in the interior membrane which envelopes the nerves . . . . By this hypothesis, I believe that there ought not to be any branch of the auditory nerve . . . but only an extension and distribution of the membrane which envelopes it internally." See item V-9, p. 489. For a discussion of Mariotte's presentations on the ear to the Paris

In 1699, John Herbert sent the Society a lengthy Latin paper on the anatomy of the ear written by the French physician Raymond Vieussens. Herbert makes it clear that Vieussens' opinions differ from those of Du Verney, that the document has been sent at Vieussens' strong request, and that he, Herbert, is not at all convinced of its accuracy. Herbert cautions: "Pray have it carefully examined before you give it to be printed, for probably here may be a french quarrel, and your Testimony and approbation wont fail to be mentioned."[118] He recommends that English experts such as the physician Edward Tyson be consulted, "for . . . here may be a French Trick, and he [Vieussens] may send you what wont bear printing in France."[119] The minutes of March 15, 1699 record that Tyson was asked to review the work.[120]

The Society did, indeed, publish Vieussens' essay in the *Transactions* of 1699,[121] and received further correspondence from him fifteen years later at the time his *Traité sur la structure de l'oreille* appeared. In a letter of 1714, Vieussens attempted to prove the existence of animal spirits which function in conveying sensations, such as sound, to the brain. As the Society's summary translation of his letter states:

> By Animal Spirit [Vieussens] understands, a substance of a Nature near that of Ethereal Matter which causes sensation on the mind, and is the principall cause of all the motions of the Parts of the body both liquid and solid.[122]

Vieussens' treatise of 1714 was apparently not reviewed. A number of years earlier, however, the Society had published a critique of another book on the ear by the Bolognese anatomist Antonio Maria Valsalva.[123] Valsalva's work elaborates on that by Du Verney and is especially noteworthy for its description

---

academy, see Cohen, *Music in the French Royal Academy*, p. 12.

[118] See item V-24, p. 373.

[119] Ibid.

[120] See item X-59.

[121] Item I-46.

[122] See item II-60 (V.48), p. 12.

[123] Item I-54. Valsalva's *De aure humana tractatus* had been published one year earlier.

of a "'zona cochleae' ... , his name for the membranous spiral lamina."[124]

Later articles on the ear include a communication from Archibald Adams containing an observation of a membrane covering the stirrup (1707),[125] an hypothesis by Edmund Halley that there must be a valve near the ear drum (1722),[126] and a paper by Job Baster on a "discovery of a process of the malleus" (1742).[127] Baster's claims of discovery were challenged by the physician Robert Nesbitt, who asserted that Baster's "process" was, in fact, the manubrium, which had been described over a century earlier.[128]

In 1799 Everard Home delivered the annual Croonian lecture on the "Structure and Uses of the Membrana Tympani of the Ear," and in 1805 Anthony Carlisle published a paper on the stapes, the smallest bone in the middle ear.[129] Both authors compare the ears of humans with those of various animals. Home, for example, first examined the tympanic membrane in elephants because the animal's size rendered the physiological features more easily observable. The author concentrates his attention on the function of the muscles associated with the membrane:

> The membrana tympani is stretched and relaxed by the action of the muscles of the malleus . . . . It is stretched, in order to bring the radiated muscle of the membrane itself into a state capable of acting . . . . When the membrane is relaxed, the radiated muscle cannot act with any effect, and external tremors make less accurate impressions.[130]

Home compares the ear drum to a monochord "of which the membrana tympani is the string; the tensor muscle the screw, giving the necessary tension to make the string perfom its proper scale of vibrations; and the radiated muscle acting

---

[124] Wever and Lawrence, *Physicological Acoustics*, p. 9.

[125] Item I-57.

[126] Item III-28

[127] Item IV-3.

[128] See item IV-4.

[129] See items I-120 and I-128. Home delivered lectures in this endowed series nineteen times from 1790 until 1829, presenting papers on muscular motion, the ear, the eye, the blood, the brain, etc.

[130] See item I-120, p. 11

upon the membrane like the moveable bridge . . . ."[131] He concludes that accuracy of musical perception is a function of the degree of perfection in the working of these muscles:

> The difference between a musical ear and one which is too imperfect to distinguish the different notes in music, will appear to arise entirely from the greater or less nicety with which the muscle of the malleus renders the membrane capable of being truly adjusted. If the tension be perfect, all the variations produced by the action of the radiated muscle will be equally correct, and the ear truly musical; but, if the first adjustment is imperfect, although the actions of the radiated muscle may still produce infinite variations, none of them will be correct: the effect . . . will be similar to that produced by playing upon a musical instrument which is not in tune.[132]

Home emphasizes that training and environment are important factors in refining a musical ear, and that the perfection of the muscles may be improved by exposure to music, or weakened by various illnesses or injuries. In demonstration of this assertion, he relates several case studies in which musical perception was impaired or even improved by medical conditions.

Home's case studies are supplemented by two additional articles published in 1800 and 1801 by another surgeon, Astley Cooper, who describes a method of restoring hearing by making a small hole in the tympanic membrane in cases where deafness is caused by a blocked tube. For this work, Cooper was awarded the prestigious Copley medal in 1801.[133]

Medical discussions that include cures for certain types of hearing disorders and deafness date back to the early years of the Society. For example, in a letter by Robert Plot dated 1683, the author proposes restoring hearing by exposure to loud bells;[134] in 1685, Daubeney Turberville described the case of a woman whose hearing was restored after she fell from a horse;[135] and at a meeting on November 17, 1703, several of the Fellows discussed the effect of

---

[131] Ibid.

[132] Ibid., p. 12

[133] See items I-122, I-123, I-126, and X-113. The Copley medal was established in 1736 and was awarded annually.

[134] Item V-8.

[135] Item II-47.

drinking bath waters in curing deafness (see Plate 11).[136] Later references include an article by Archibald Cleland in 1741, which deals with medical instruments used to cure some types of hearing loss,[137] and one by Jonathan Wathen in 1755 on a method of removing an obstruction from a blocked Eustacian tube.[138] In a review of Benjamin Franklin's *Experiments and Observations on Electricity* (1751), published in the *Transactions* in 1751, William Watson mentions the use of electricity in restoring hearing.[139] Electricity's effect on the sense of hearing is also discussed in a letter to the Society from Alexander Volta in 1800.[140]

Anatomical discussions of the human voice are, curiously, much more rare than are those of the ear. The only work of note, in fact, is a dissertation by one Colet de Chaulet, sent from Paris in 1745, and a review of this same dissertation by Thomas Stack, a member of the Society.[141] In his letter (which was not printed), Chaulet refutes new theories on voice production recently presented to the Paris Academy by Antoine Ferrein, supporting instead older theories by Denis Dodart.[142] Chaulet disagrees with Ferrein's description of the physiology and the functioning of the larynx, particularly objecting to his analogies between the glottis and stringed instruments. Chaulet presents several specific counter-arguments and asserts that the critical factor in voice production is the degree of opening of the glottis, rather than in its vibrations as with a string.

Sound perception and production by animals also interested the Society, in particular, hearing in fish. In 1740, Jacob Theodore Klein, a zoologist, published a treatise on fish in which he described bones that, he claimed, served as their auditory mechanism; the work was favorably reviewed in the

---

[136] Item X-62.

[137] Item I-66.

[138] Item I-87.

[139] Item I-83.

[140] Item I-124.

[141] Items IV-5 and IV-7.

[142] See Cohen, *Music in the French Royal Academy,* pp. 20-21 and 35-36, and Cohen and Miller, *Music in the Paris Academy of Sciences,* pp. 26-28 and 33.

Transactions in 1742.[143] Three years later, Henry Baker wrote to the Society's secretary Martin Folkes, imparting information about an eel that died as a result of being exposed to loud music.[144] However, the ability of fish to perceive sound was not completely accepted, and in 1748 two conflicting articles appeared in the *Transactions*. One, by William Arderon, concluded that what seemed to be a sense of hearing was instead highly developed senses of sight and feeling; the second article, by the physician Richard Brocklesby, reviewed a work by Klein that advocated the opposite viewpoint.[145] The debate was still alive in 1782 when the anatomist John Hunter published an article in the *Transactions* which described the organ of hearing in various types of fish as comprising "three curved tubes, all of which unite with one another."[146]

Other articles on sound production and reception by animals include those on hearing in whales (Joseph Ames, 1750) and in dogs (Sloane, 1699); on hearing and singing of birds (Allen Moulin, 1687-88, Henry Nicholson, 1712, Daines Barrington, 1773, Edward Jenner, 1788); and even on the song of the cicada (Giovanni Battista Felici, 1717).[147] Barrington's lengthy discussion of bird songs is particularly notable, the author asserting that such songs are learned, not innate. Barrington describes the warblings of a large number of species and even appends a musical composition "for two piping bullfinches," which is printed in the *Transactions*. The author himself was an amateur musician, who three years earlier had presented another paper to the Society -- this one, an eyewitness account of Mozart at age 8.[148]

---

[143] Item I-67.

[144] See below, p. 34.

[145] See items I-77 and I-78.

[146] See item I-108, p. 381.

[147] See the following items: Ames, IV-9; Sloane, X-58; Moulin, I-34 and II-48; Nicholson, II-59; Barrington, I-99; Jenner, I-112; and Felici, VI-22.

[148] See below, pp. 41-42.

THE POWER OF MUSIC:
MUSIC AS MEDICINE; THE MUSIC OF THE ANCIENTS

The Society actively followed developments in the field of medicine, including theories on the curative powers of music. Of particular interest was the role of music and dance in curing tarantula bites. Henry Oldenburg actively pursued the matter with many of his correspondents: the subject is discussed in letters between Oldenburg and Martin Lister in York (1671 and 1672), John Dodington and Thomas Cornelio in Italy (1671 and 1672), and John Beale in Somerset (1672).[149] It also figures prominently in several book reviews published in the *Transactions,* such as those of Moyse Charas, *Suite des nouvelles expériences sur la vipère* (1671), Paolo Boccone, *Museo di fisica . . .* (1699), and Richard Mead, *Mechanical Account of Poysons* (1702).[150] In theory, the bite of the tarantula found in the region of Apulia in southern Italy induced a delirium, which could only be cured by the performance of certain tunes. (The same spiders, transported out of Apulia, were found to be harmless.) When the proper tunes were played, the stricken person felt compelled to dance and "sweat out the malady."[151] Furthermore, once bitten, the symptoms tended to recur annually in the summer season, and though less intense, they nevertheless required the same cure.[152] Charas relates the tale of a Neapolitan soldier, who, each year

> began to dance, and would hear without interruption the Violins, which the Officers of that Regiment caused to be play'd for him out of charity; to which he answer'd continually, keeping his time very well, without being tired, during three daies, eating and drinking without interrupting his dance, and being very impatient at any discontinuance of the play of the Violins.[153]

---

[149] See items I-8, I-11, II-19, II-25, II-30, and II-38.

[150] The reviews were published in 1672, 1699, and 1703, respectively. See items I-12, I-44, and I-48.

[151] Item I-48, p. 1322.

[152] For a history of the malady, see Henry E. Sigerist, "The Story of Tarantism," in *Music and Medicine* (New York: H. Schumann, 1948), pp. 96-116.

[153] See item I-12, p. 4076.

Mead explains that the cure worked

> not only by exciting to those motions that help . . . by Sweat and Evacuations,
> but as the harmonically Vibrating Air, by immediate contact affects the
> contractile Membranes with such a determinate force, especially those of the
> Ear, and thereby of the Brain, which assists the contraction of the Fibrils, [that
> it] prevents a beginning Coagulation.[154]

Incidences of the "disease" gradually declined during the eighteenth century, as
did the belief in music's curative powers. In 1770, Dominico Cirillo wrote to
the Society:

> the surprizing cure of the bite of the Tarantula, by music, has not the least
> truth in it; . . . it is only an invention of the people, who want to get a little
> money, by dancing when they say the tarantism begins.[155]

Other medically-related articles include case studies of a woman who
sang only when in a delirium (1747) and of the eel that died after hearing loud
cello music (1745).[156] The latter is based on a report from G. L. Bruni about a
large river eel in a tub, who

> was brisk and lively[;] but [when] two servants . . . [began] playing very loud
> on the Violoncello, at the Distance of about 5 Feet from the Tub, the Eel
> began immediately to appear uneasy and restless, flinging itself violently from
> side to side, and in half an Hour's Time it was found quite dead.[157]

Baker describes other effects of music on man and animals, including a report
on a dog that experienced convulsions at the sound of a drum.

Even music's effect on plants has a place in the proceedings; in a letter
dated 1728, J. I. Carrillo, physician to the king of Tunis, describes an African
plant of the genus Verbascum, whose flowers respond to different types of
music. According to Carrillo, when an Arab musician plays in a tragic mode

---

[154] Item I-48, p. 1323. Mead apparently relied heavily on Giorgio Baglivi's *Dissertatio de
anatome, morsue, et effectibus tarantulae* (1695).

[155] Item I-97, p. 237. Travelling bands of musicians apparently extracted healthy fees in return
for "curing" the disease.

[156] See items I-75 and IV-6.

[157] Item IV-6, p. 1.

(the *"tonus mermus,"* which "imitates the tragic howling of Melpomene"),[158] the plant's flowers fade, close and droop, but "to high strains," they are erect and lively. Although the author offers speculations on the cause of this phenomenon, he acknowledges that he cannot develop a theory in keeping with known scientific information.

Robert Hooke deals with the reputed miraculous effects of music in an unpublished paper sent to the Society after his death by William Derham.[159] The work is undated, but evidence points to its having been written ca. 1676.[160] Hooke describes the effects produced by music on human emotions and "in the curing and working on the parts of ye body"[161] as derived from both Biblical and historical traditions and from current beliefs. He also discusses the nature of sound and the ear's reception of it as

a tremulous motion of the drum & organ of the ear, excited by the like motion of the sonorous medium, wch received its motion from the Sounding Body.[162]

Also included in Hooke's paper is information on the length and tension of a string in relation to pitch, and on sympathetic vibration. The author attributes the wondrous effects of music to the great variety of possible melodies, rhythmic figures, dynamics, and harmonic structures.

On the other hand, John Wallis, in a paper published in the *Transactions* of 1698, suggests that the reported miraculous effects of Greek music are exaggerated and misunderstood.[163] He attributes the tales of music's power to literary embellishment, the simplicity of the ancient people, and the inclusion of poetry and dance in discussions of music.

---

[158] Item II-63, p. 3.

[159] See item III-29. The essay is edited with commentary in Penelope Gouk, "The Role of Acoustics and Music Theory in the Scientific Work of Robert Hooke," *Annals of Science* 37 (1980): 573-605.

[160] Ibid.

[161] Ibid., p. 600.

[162] Ibid., p. 601.

[163] Item I-41.

Nevertheless, the Society showed obvious interest in Greek music in general. Articles on the subject include references to instruments depicted in ancient art works and a discussion of a musical treatise by Philodemus (all of which were unearthed in the archeological exploration of the city of Herculaneum, ca. 1750),[164] speculations on ancient instruments,[165] and several lengthy papers on Greek theory, including one by John Christopher Pepusch in 1746 and another by Sir Francis Haskins Eyles-Stiles in 1760.[166] The last named piece, an extensive explanation of Greek modal theory relying heavily on Ptolemy, was praised by both Burney and Hawkins,[167] and was apparently considered very important by the Society. In addition to its publication in the *Transactions*, an extensive summary is entered in the *Journal Book*, and several manuscript copies of the article may be found in the archives. In addition to these papers, John Wallis translated important Greek musical treatises into Latin as early as 1699,[168] and several book reviews published in the early years of the *Transactions* deal with ancient music. Of particular note are those on William Wotton's *Reflections upon Ancient and Modern Learning* (1694) and on Isaac Voss' *De poematum cantu* (1673).[169] Voss' view is that ancient music is more powerful than modern in "moving our senses," for in the latter the words cannot be understood and the rhythm is at variance with the text accents. Restoring the ancient power of music may only be accomplished, in Voss' opinion, by a more thorough application of poetic accents to musical compositions.

---

[164] See items I-81, I-82, I-85, I-86, and I-88 through 91. For a discussion of Philodemus' *De musica*, see Warren Anderson, *Ethos and Education in Greek Music* (Cambridge: Harvard University Press, 1966), pp. 153-76.

[165] See above, pp. 24-25.

[166] Items I-73 and I-92.

[167] See John Hawkins, *A General History of the Science and Practice of Music* (1776; reprint of the 1853 ed. with introduction by Charles Cudworth, New York: Dover Publications, 1963), p. 49, and Charles Burney, *A General History of Music* (reprint of the 2nd ed., 1789, ed. Frank Mercer, New York: Dover Publications, 1957), vol. 1, pp. 58-61.

[168] See above, p. 7.

[169] Items I-36 and I-17.

WESTERN MUSIC THEORY

Archival documents dealing with contemporaneous musical theory, though few in number, are nevertheless of consequence. Particularly notable are those that relate to the work of two composer-theorists, John Birchensha and Jean-Philippe Rameau. Birchensha's name first appears in the minutes in 1662, when two papers of his were presented to the Society (on April 16 and November 12), the second of which was critiqued by William Brouncker.[170] The earliest document by Birchensha preserved in the Society's archives, however, is a letter, dated April 26, 1664, which outlines the contents of a projected treatise on the mathematical and practical aspects of music.[171] In it, Birchensha promises to provide accurate rules for finding proportions of intervals and string length measurements for all tones within the octave, following the model of Pythagoras. He also describes his intention of placing all of the possible tones employed in music into a "complete scale," which he planned to present to the Royal Society along with directions on its use. On the practical side, Birchensha asserts that he will systematize the rules of composition and provide a method by which anyone can learn to compose quickly and easily without the use of an instrument. He considered that composing at an instrument was "a low and mechanick way. But to compose by a Rule, is . . . more Noble, artificial, and commendable . . . ."[172] He promised to discuss composition in one and more parts, counterpoint, scoring music, setting words to music, etc. The Society appointed a committee to examine Birchensha's work and to "consider . . . ways to encourage and promote his design and study."[173]

From this time forward, Birchensha repeatedly predicted the publication of his "Syntagma musicae," but the treatise did not materialize. However, what

---

[170] See items X-2 and X-4. Two other anonymous papers presented on Feb. 5 and July 12 of this same year might possibly have been by Birchensha. See Birch, vol. 1, pp. 75 and 87, and Gouk, "Music in the . . . Early Royal Society," p. 82.

[171] See item V-3.

[172] Item V-3, p. 168.

[173] The Committee was established on April 20; Birchensha's paper was read on April 27. See items X-10 and X-11.

appears to be an early draft of the work is found among the *Boyle Papers*. Entitled "A Compendious Discourse of the Principles of the Practicall and Mathematicall Partes of Musick," it was written by Birchensha "for the use of Robert Boyle" (see Plate 9).[174] The work contains thirteen chapters on practical matters, twenty-one on mathematical theory, and a supplementary section with instructions on "How to make any kind of Tune or Ayre without the helpe of the Voice or any other Musicall Instrument." Among the practical matters covered are the expected discussions of the elements of music: the staff, note names, modes, rhythm, solmization, etc.[175]

The two most novel aspects of Birchensha's theories are the "grand scale" and the rules for composition. The "Compendious Discourse" sheds some light on both of these. The scale appears to be a temperament system, Birchensha advocating different tunings for enharmonically equivalent pitches in order to arrive at mathematically perfect intervals. He recommends extending the circle of fifths beyond 12 tones by continuing to add pure fifths until every note is double sharp and double flat:

> For the completeing of all Consonant and Dissonant Intervalls in All keyes flatt and sharp: (viz. Ab A A# - Bb B B# - Cb C C# - Db D D# - Eb E E# - Fb F F# - Gb G G# -) it will be of absolute necessity to make all the 7 Natural keyes - double flatt: and double sharp and then the keyes which will complete a perfect scale of musick in the diatonic and permixed (commonly called the chromatic) genus, will be -
> Abb Ab A A# Ax - Bbb Bb B B# Bx - Cbb Cb C C# Cx - Dbb Db D D# Dx - Ebb Eb E E# Ex - Fbb Fb F F# Fx - Gbb Gb G G# Gx . . . .[176]

Nonetheless, the author implies that not all of the 21 keys given above are necessary. In an earlier section of the "Discourse," he presents a table of all of the consonant and dissonant intervals "in all keyes practicable by our instruments."[177] Only 25 tones are included here, instead of the 35 in the

---

[174] See item VIII-7.

[175] Birchensha presents the four-syllable solmization system typical in England at the time and explains time signatures in terms of tempos with references to dances.

[176] "Compendious Discourse," ch. 9, p. 20.

[177] Ibid., Chapter 13, p. 7.

complete system listed above.[178] Birchensha does not discuss the practical problems of such a system, and his work met with mixed reviews.[179]

Birchensha's easy method of composition, as given in the "Compendious Discourse," deals only with the creation of a single melodic line. He provides guidelines for constructing melodies; includes musical notation of "passing," "formall," and "final" closes; provides examples of how to vary a melody by rhythmic diminution, inversion, or other means; and offers samples of poor melodic constructions.[180]

Although the "Discourse" is not dated, it can be assumed to have been written before 1673, for by this time Birchensha had expanded the work to include still a third portion on the "Philosophical" aspects of music. A notice in the *Transactions* of this year promises publication "on or before March 24, 1674,"[181] and a document in the *Classified Papers* summarizes the contents of the three sections.[182] This document shows similarities to, but significant revisions from, the "Compendious Discourse." With the exception of the "Discourse" and a few additional documents related to it in the British Library,

---

[178] The practical keys are: A Bb B C C# D Eb E F F# G and Ab. The intervals given are the m2, M2, m3, M3, P4, "semidiapente" (= diminished 5th), tritone (= augmented 4th), P5, m6, M6, m7, "semidiapason" (= diminished octave), M7, and P8. Of the 35 tones listed above, this chart includes all but these: Ax, Bx, Cbb, Cx, Dbb, Dx, Ex, Fbb, Gbb, and Gx. For a detailed discussion of Birchensha's theories, see Gouk, "Music in the . . . Early Royal Society," ch. 4.

[179] As early as February 24, 1662, Samuel Pepys (who studied composition with Birchensha for two months from January 13 to February 27 of that year) says he has seen Birchensha's "great card of the body of musique," but doesn't find it as useful as the theorist claimed. See Pepys, *Diary*, vol. 3, pp. 34-35.

[180] A few composition rules by Birchensha with examples in two parts, as compiled by Silas Taylor, may be found in British Library Add. Ms. 4910, fols. 39-61. No record of his rules for composition in more than two parts has come to light, although the theorist promised such rules as part of his book (see footnote 181). It may be for this reason that John Evelyn notes in his diary (August 3, 1664) that Birchensha has invented "a mathematical way of composure very extraordinary. True as to the exact rules of art, but without much harmonie" (Evelyn, *Diary*, vol. 3, p. 377).

[181] See item I-16. Birchensha promises rules not only "for making Airy tunes of all sorts," but also for composing in 2-7 parts, assuring readers that they will be able to write in two parts in two months, in three parts in three months, and so forth.

[182] Item III-12. This document represents at least a portion of a presentation Birchensha made to the Society on February 10, 1676. See item X-35. It is clear that the book was not yet published at this time and some of the Fellows questioned whether his theories were, in fact, new. The Society urged him "to finish this work, or at least to publish this system with an explanation thereof." See item X-35, p. 296.

however,[183] no completed treatise has surfaced.

Rameau's relationship to the Royal Society was much more extensive than scholars have heretofore imagined, spanning nearly a quarter-century, during which time he sent three of his treatises to that body for review. The *Nouveau système* was, in fact, favorably critiqued by Brook Taylor, himself an amateur musician. The review was read at a meeting on January 18, 1728, but not published.[184] On August 12, 1737, Rameau sent the *Génération harmonique* to then-president Hans Sloane, and on February 26, 1750, he sent a copy of the *Démonstration du principe de l'harmonie*.[185] There is no record in the Society's proceedings that either of these later treatises was formally reviewed, although in both cases the *Journal Book* reports that one of the Fellows was assigned the task. (The *Génération harmonique* was referred to James Hamilton, Lord Paisley, and the *Démonstration* to John Christopher Pepusch.)[186] In the case of the *Démonstration*, Rameau followed his initial request with a second letter, nine months later, in which he provides a 12-page summary of his arguments with marginal annotations referring to specific pages in the treatise, in hopes of exciting the curiosity of the Fellows (see Plate 5).[187] This letter contains several paragraphs that later appear *verbatim* in his *Nouvelles réflexions* of 1752.[188] Among these is Rameau's well-known reference to the authority of Isaac Newton,[189] apparently included in order to stimulate a review of his work by the Fellows.

---

[183] British Library Add. Mss. 4388 and 4910. The former contains John Pell's calculations of Birchensha's scale. See Gouk, "Music in the . . . Early Royal Society," ch. 4 for discussion. For Ms. 4910, see footnote 180.

[184] The original document is filed in the *Classified Papers* and was copied into the *Register Book*. See items III-30 and VI-25, and the article on Taylor in *New Grove* (which mentions the *Register Book* copy but not the original document, and gives the year as 1727).

[185] See items II-69 and IV-8.

[186] Paisley was a student of Pepusch (see below). Pepusch was elected to the Society on June 13, 1745.

[187] Item IV-11.

[188] The entire letter, together with Brook Taylor's review and Rameau's earlier correspondence to the Society, may be found in Leta Miller, "Rameau and the Royal Society: New Letters and Documents," *Music and Letters* 66, no. 1 (January 1985): 19-33.

[189] The reference cites Newton's comparisons between sound and light. See Miller, ibid. Newton was president of the Society from 1703 to 1727.

A few years after Taylor's review of Rameau's *Nouveau système,* another treatise was similarly reviewed: *A Treatise on Harmony, Containing the Chief Rules for Composing in 2, 3, and 4 Parts* . . . .[190] The critique was read to the Society on February 17, 1732, and, like Taylor's paper, the original document was filed among the *Classified Papers* and a copy entered into the *Register Book.* The copy (but not the original) identifies the author of the treatise as James Lord Paisley, although the book has generally been attributed to John Christopher Pepusch. The confusion is partly clarified by John Hawkins, who suggests that Paisley, a student of Pepusch, in fact wrote the first edition of the treatise (1730). In the second edition (1731), according to Hawkins, Pepusch added musical examples.

Other treatises reviewed by the Society include: Thomas Salmon's *An Essay to the Advancement of Musick* (1672),[191] William Holder's *A Treatise of the Natural Grounds and Principles of Harmony* (1694), Pietro Mengoli's *Musica speculativa* (1674), and Francis North's *A Philosophical Essay of Music* (1677).[192]

COMPOSERS

Two articles published in the *Transactions* concern musicians of the time, both of whom were child prodigies. The Society's interest seems to have centered on the extraordinary minds of the children, rather than on their musical production. The first of these papers is an eyewitness account by Daines Barrington of Mozart at age 8. The author tells us that he presented the child with a manuscript duet having an accompaniment of two violins and bass, that Mozart sight-read the opening instrumental sinfonia, as well as the bass and one voice part of the duet (adding the violin lines as needed), and that, at the same time, he corrected his father, who occasionally erred as he sang the lower part.

---

[190] See item III-31.

[191] Salmon studied with Birchensha, who wrote the preface to the treatise.

[192] See items I-10, I-35, I-21, and I-25, respectively.

Barrington then recounts how young Wolfgang improvised several arias in Italian, in an appropriate operatic style. The author compares Mozart's ability to that of a child who "was directed to read five lines at once, in four of which the letters of the alphabet were to have different powers . . ." (a reference to the different clefs), and that furthermore, the child was reading "a capital speech in Shakespeare never seen before, and yet read . . . with all the pathetic energy of a Garrick . . . ," all the while "reading, with a glance of his eye, three different comments on this speech . . . , one . . . in Greek, the second in Hebrew, and the third in Etruscan characters."[193]

This event took place in June 1765, but the article was not communicated to the Society until 1769. The delay was apparently due to Barrington's initial disbelief of the child's age; in the succeeding few years, however, he was able to verify Mozart's birthdate from records in Salzburg.

The second account of an extraordinary child musician is Charles Burney's description of William Crotch. Burney discusses Crotch's precocious abilities in improvising compositions on the organ, and even compares Crotch to Mozart -- noting, however, that the former lacked the role models and early training given to the latter. Burney himself was elected a Fellow of the Society in 1773, and the organization obtained many of his books for its library.[194]

MISCELLANEOUS ARTICLES

A number of items in the Society's proceedings deal with music as part of general discussions of other topics. For example, in a paper by Edward Thornycroft on "The Doctrine of Combinations and Alternations,"[195] the author cites a musical example: how to find the number of melodies possible on certain instruments with fixed ranges. Along the same lines, William Petty discusses music and sound among the various uses of duplicate and subduplicate

---

[193] Item I-95, pp. 58-59.

[194] See, for example, items I-100, I-104, I-109, I-110, and I-115.

[195] Item I-53.

proportions in a discourse he presented to the Fellows in 1674.[196]

Musical topics are also discussed in articles devoted to manuscripts or printing. Noteworthy among these are an essay by Humfrey Wanley (1705) presenting guidelines for judging the age of manuscripts,[197] communications from George Lewis (1697) and Wanley (1701) describing manuscripts from Greece and the Near East which contain hymns and anthems,[198] two catalogs of oriental and Sanscrit manuscripts presented to the Society by Sir William and Lady Jones (1798-99),[199] and an article by Wanley on the history of printing (1703)[200] which mentions the publishing of songs. In 1751 the French Jesuit Antoine Gaubil sent ten Chinese tunes to the Society.[201] Although the title given to Gaubil's communication in the manuscript index of the *Letters and Papers* reads "Of Chinese Music," this title is misleading; Gaubil's letters are generally unrelated to music except for the appended melodies (see Plate 6). Four of the ten tunes he sent had already appeared in Jean-Baptiste du Halde's *Description géographique, historique, chronologique, politique et physique de l'Empire de la Chine et de la Tartarie chinoise* (1735).[202] The first one has become particularly well known through its adaptation by Carl Maria von Weber in his *Turandot* and its subsequent use by Paul Hindemith in the *Symphonic Metamorphoses*.

Among the more obscure contributions to music in archival documents is an article by the writer Cave Beck, who describes the building of symbolic "houses" (after Bacon) to aid in memory, included among which is a "Brasse

---

[196] Item VI-10.

[197] Item I-55.

[198] Items I-42 and X-61.

[199] Items I-118 and I-119.

[200] Item III-17.

[201] Item IV-14.

[202] See Ysia Tchen, *La musique chinoise en France au XVIIIe siècle* (Paris: Publications Orientalistes de France, 1974), pp. 33-41. Tchen remarks that the tunes are incorrectly notated in Du Halde and presents a revised version with all tones a third lower. Interestingly, Gaubil's version of the same tunes shows three of the four a third *higher* and the fourth a step higher than Du Halde.

Musick House."[203] Yet another is a metaphysical discussion by J. de Cordié (1734),[204] who identifies five basic "substances" of which our world is comprised: "sec, eau, aer, lumière, et feu," as well as five "modes" in which these substances are found: "mineral, vegetable, reptile, volatil," and "génie ou homme." Musical instruments are classified according to their relationship to these five modes and substances, and the author uses various analogies to support the primacy of the number five, including the five senses, the five vowels, five basic geometrical shapes, and the musical triad (which outlines the notes of a fifth). Of the seven musical tones, Cordié claims that only five are basic -- ut, re, mi, fa, and sol, corresponding to the five vowels (u = ut, a = fa, etc.; see Plate 3).

Other items dealing with the relation of music and language include the review of Voss' *De poematum cantu* cited above (1673),[205] which recommends the coordination of musical rhythm with text accentuation; several letters from Antoine Court de Gebelin, who employs musical analogies in comparing various languages with each other (1768);[206] and a letter from the rector Richard Roach, who advocates an "improvement of rhetorical elocution" by establishing a notation for speech similar to that of music (1722).[207] Roach asserts that a speech or poem can be

> Prick'd down in Musical Notes reduced to Mood and Time; with its proper Bass or other parts adapted, and may be Perform'd or pronounced with the Organ, Harpsichord or other Instrument according in Perfect Harmony.[208]

---

[203] Item III-23.

[204] Item II-68.

[205] Item I-17

[206] Items IV-23 and IV-24

[207] See item II-61. A system for doing so was devised by Joshua Steele and presented in his *Essay towards Establishing the Melody and Measure of Speech* (published 1775; a second edition, *Prosodia rationalis*, was published in 1779). These books were presented to the Royal Society in 1776 and 1780, respectively (see items I-104 and I-107), but were not reviewed.

[208] Item II-61, p. 384.

SUMMARY

Examination of the items cataloged in the present index reveals that the greatest interest in musical topics at the Royal Society occurred within the first fifty years of its activity. Of the relevant letters, papers, and *Journal Book* references from this time, the musical subject given the most attention was acoustics: experiments and presentations on the nature and speed of sound, on vibrations of strings and of solid bodies, and on tuning systems. Significantly, the early minutes, although sketchy and brief, do not merely indicate that papers were read; they also describe demonstrations at the meetings, including, at times, musical performances. Other areas of interest in the early period include instruments (particularly the speaking trumpet), the anatomy of the ear and the process of sound reception, and the relationship of music to medicine (particularly that concerning the legend of tarantism). Furthermore, John Birchensha's close association with the Society resulted in a number of theoretical subjects being discussed during its formative years.

The Society's interest in musical topics declined gradually during the latter half of the eighteenth century, although bursts of activity were at times stimulated by external events or by the particular concerns of individual Fellows. The number of articles on music theory during the period 1725-50, for example, certainly arose at least in part from Rameau's repeated appeals for review of his books by the Society, and from the election as Fellows to that body of two musicians, James Lord Paisley and John Christopher Pepusch. The archeological dig at Herculaneum around mid-century unearthed quite by accident a musical treatise as well as art works depicting Greek instruments, and in the last quarter of the century, interest in musical topics may have been stimulated by Charles Burney's election to the organization in 1773.

Although the Society does not appear to have had any systematic approach to solving musical or acoustical problems during the 150 years covered by the present study, it did provide the greater scientific community with a forum for presenting significant papers and experiments dealing with such problems. It also established a means for recording and disseminating the results of its deliberations, which generally led to a more accurate understanding of acoustical science, of the auditory process, and of musical developments in theory and temperament. As a group, the papers of the Royal Society cataloged herein serve to broaden our perception of the role played by music in the scientific world of the seventeenth and eighteenth centuries.

I. PHILOSOPHICAL TRANSACTIONS (PT)

The primary publication of the Royal Society, the *Philosophical Transactions*, was initiated in 1665 by the first secretary, Henry Oldenburg, who published approximately one issue per month until his death in 1677. The early volumes each contain between five and ten articles on various topics, as well as book reviews, letters, and notices of events of interest to the greater scientific community. Issues were normally bound into yearly volumes, at times with inconsistent pagination. After Oldenburg's death, publication was sporadic for a number of years. Nehemiah Grew edited only six issues in 1678, after which the task was assumed by Robert Hooke. Rather than continuing Oldenburg's title, Hooke began his own journal, *The Philosophical Collections*, which comprised seven issues spanning the years 1679 to April 1682. The *Philosophical Collections* are sometimes bound into volume 12 of the *Transactions*. In 1683, the *Transactions* were resumed under the editorship of Robert Plot and, except for a hiatus from 1687 through 1691, thereafter appeared on a regular basis. Responsibility for their publication was assumed by subsequent secretaries until 1751, when a committee of the Society was officially appointed to oversee them. The editors of the *Transactions* were the following:

Date	Volume No.	Editor
1665-77	1-11	Henry Oldenburg
1678	12	Oldenburg/Nehemiah Grew
1679-82	*Philosophical Collections*	Robert Hooke
1683-84	13-14	Robert Plot
1685	15	William Musgrave
1686-87	16	Edmund Halley
1688-91	no issues published	
1692-94	17-18	Richard Waller
1695-1713	19-28	Hans Sloane
1714-19	29-30	Edmund Halley
1720-June 1727	31-34	James Jurin
July 1727-28	35	William Rutty
1729-50	36-46	Cromwell Mortimer
1751ff.	47ff.	Committee of the Society

There exist subject and author indices for the *Transactions* for the period covered by the present study: one for vols. 1-70 (1667-1780, published by Paul Maty in 1787), and a second for vols. 71-110 (1781-1820, with an additional section for volumes up to 1830).

The *Transactions* were reprinted in various sets of abridgments beginning in 1705. Of particular note among these is a 1749 publication (vols. 1-3, a 5th edition by John Lowthorp, and vols. 4-5, a 3rd edition by Henry Jones), which includes translations of the Latin papers into English, a sign of the increasing necessity for use of the vernacular in scientific work (a trend seen also in the *Early Letters* of the time).

This section of the present catalog is organized according to the publication dates of the *Transactions*. Articles were generally printed within a short time after they were written or presented to the Society. One notable exception to this, however, is Southwell's letter on whispering places and echoes, written in 1661 but not published until nearly a century later in 1746 (see item I-72).

Information in the following catalog includes: author and title; volume, issue, and page numbers in the *Transactions;* publication date of the issue; and the date on which the paper was read at the Society, if known. This last information appears in the *Transactions* only for the later papers; for earlier listings, the information is generally derived from references in the *Journal Book.*

1668

I-1. (Book notice): Accademia del Cimento, *Saggi di Naturali Esperienze* (Florence, 1667). PT: vol. 3, no. 33 (March 16, 1667/8), p. 640.

Announcement of the publication with a listing of topics covered, but no discussion. Item 11 on sound.

I-2. (Book review): W[olferdus] Sengwerdius, [*Tractatus physicus*] De Tarantula (Leiden, 1668). PT: vol. 3, no. 34 (April 13, 1668), pp. 660-62.

Explanation of cure for tarantula bites by music and dance.

I-3. Holder, William.
An Account of an Experiment concerning Deafness [read April 23, 1668]. PT: vol. 3, no. 35 (May 18, 1668), pp. 665-68.
Manuscript copy: RB VI-8

Anatomical discussion of function of tympanum and bones in ear, and speculation as to one cause of hearing loss.

I-4. (Book notice): Renatus Des Cartes, *Epistolae*, pts. 1 & 2 (London: 1668). PT: vol. 3, no. 40 (Oct. 19, 1668), p. 810.

Publication announcement of Latin translation of René Descartes' letters with brief listing of topics (including music), but no discussion.

1670

I-5. Wallis, John.
A letter . . . to Robert Boyle Esq., concerning the said Doctor's Essay of Teaching a person Dumb and Deaf to speak and to Understand a

Language; together with the success thereof (dated Oxford, March 14, 1661/2). PT: vol. 5, no. 61 (July 18, 1670), pp. 1087-97.
Ref.: BL VIII-2, JB X-2a

Description of teaching speech to a deaf-mute. Includes brief references to sound and to the lute. Wallis' claims refuted by William Holder and subsequently defended by Wallis. See Wallis, *A Defence of the Royal Society; And the Philosophical Transactions, Particularly those of July 1670* (London: Thomas Moore, 1678). On May 21, 1662, Wallis had brought a deaf-mute whom he had taught to speak to the Society for a demonstration (see ref.).

1671

I-6. (Book review): Antonio Molinetti, *Dissertationes Anatomicae & Pathologicae de Sensibus & eorum Organis* (Padua, 1669). PT: vol. 5, no. 67 (Jan. 16, 1670/1), pp. 2059-62.

Outlines topics covered without detailed discussion; p. 2060 on the ear and hearing.

I-7. (Book review): Academia Naturae Curiosorum, *Miscellanea Curiosa Medico Physica* (Leipzig, 1670). PT: vol. 5, no. 68 (Feb. 20, 1670/1), pp. 2077-82.

A brief discussion of articles in the first volume of *Les Ephémérides des Curieux de la Nature d'Allemagne*, published by the Academia Naturae Curiosorum. Relevant items include: p. 2079, curing deafness; p. 2081, person struck in the eye with musical string; p. 2082, man with a strange antipathy to music.

I-8. Lyster [Lister, Martin].
Some Additions of Mr. Lyster to his former Communications about Vegetable Excrescencies, and Ichneumon Wasps; together with an

Inquiry concerning Tarantula's, and a Discovery of another Musk-scented Insect (dated York, October 16 and 28, 1671) PT: vol. 6, no. 77 (Nov. 20, 1671), pp. 3002-03.
>Original: EL II-20
>Ed.: Old. no. 1800

>Poses inquiries about music appropriate to curing tarantula bites in the letter of Oct. 16.

1672

I-9. (Book review): Sam[uel] Moreland [Morland], [*Tuba stentoro-phonica*] (London, 1671). An Account of the Speaking Trumpet, as it hath been contrived and published by Sir Sam. Moreland . . . ; together with its Uses both at Sea and Land. PT: vol. 6, no. 79 (Jan. 22, 1671/2), pp. 3056-58.

>Describes a speaking trumpet invented by Morland for magnifying sound. The largest device is said to be able to carry sounds two to three miles in a favorable wind. Includes speculations on how the trumpet operates.

I-10. (Book review): Tho[mas] Salmon, *An Essay to the Advancement of Musick* (London, 1672). PT: vol. 6, no. 80 (Feb. 19, 1671/2), p. 3095.

>Short description of Salmon's book, emphasizing his proposal to reduce all clefs to one.

I-11. Cornelio, Thomas.
>An Extract of a Letter, written March 5, 1672 . . . concerning some Observations made of persons pretending to be stung by Tarantula's: English'd out of the Italian [read April 24]. PT: vol. 7, no. 83 (May 20, 1672), pp. 4066-67.
>Original: EL II-31

Ed. and trans.: Old. no. 1911a

Relates how a man, claiming to have been bitten by a tarantula, had no inclination to dance or to hear music; he died within two days.

I-12. (Book review): Moyse Charas, *Suite des nouvelles Expériences sur la Vipère, avec une Dissertation sur son Venin* (Paris, 1671). PT: vol. 7, no. 83 (May 20, 1672), pp. 4073-77.

Relates tale of soldier who experienced a recurrence of his inclination to dance and hear violin music each summer after having been bitten by a tarantula (p. 4076).

I-13. Platt, Thomas.
An Extract of a Letter . . . from Florence, August 6, 1672, concerning some Experiments, there made upon Vipers. PT: vol. 7, no. 87 (Oct. 14, 1672), pp. 5060-66.
Original: EL II-39
Ed.: Old. no. 2037

Includes a digression on Pietro Salvetti's tuning of the "Lira Viol," rendering it "wholly perfect," p. 5064.

I-14. Newton, Isaac.
Mr. Isaac Newtons Answer to some Considerations upon his Doctrine of Light and Colors. PT: vol. 7, no. 88 (Nov. 18, 1672), pp. 5084-5103.

Compares light and sound, pp. 5088 and 5091.

I-15. (Book review): Accademia [de' Gelati] di Bologna, *Prose de Signori Academici di Bologna* (Bologna, 1672). PT: vol. 7, no. 89 (Dec. 16, 1672), pp. 5125-28.

Mentions musical subjects covered, p. 5128.

1673

I-16. (Book notice): John Birchensha, *Syntagma Musicae*. PT: vol. 7, no. 90 (Jan. 20, 1672/3), pp. 5153-54.
Ref.: CP III-12, LB V-3, BP VIII-7

Announces book to be published on or before March 24, 1674, which "treats of Musick Philosophically, Mathematically, and Practically." Article describes contents, including the causes of musical sound, elements of music theory, rules of composition in 2-7 parts, an easy way for "making Airy Tunes," etc. Book apparently never printed. (Birchensha's views on the "practical" and "mathematical" parts of music are found in his "Compendious Discourse" [item VIII-7], which may be an earlier version of the "Syntagma musicae.")

I-17. (Book review): Isaacus Vossius [Isaac Voss], *De Poematum Cantu & Viribus Rythmi* (Oxford, 1673). PT: vol. 8, no. 93 (April 21, 1673), pp. 6024-30.

Extols ancient music, its various parts (harmony, words, rhythm), and its affective power; recommends careful linkage of musical rhythm to the syllable lengths of the text.

I-18. (Book review): Ignace-Gaston Pardies, *La Statique, ou La Science des Forces Mouvantes* (Paris, 1673). PT: vol. 8, no. 94 (May 19, 1673), pp. 6042-46.

The second of a projected six-part work on mechanics; briefly reviews contents of later volumes planned, including the nature of vibration and sound transmission.

I-19. Newton, [Isaac].

Mr. Newtons Answer to . . . [a] Letter further explaining his Theory of Light and Colors, and particularly that of Whiteness . . . . PT: vol. 8, no. 96 (July 21, 1673), pp. 6087-92.

Brief reference to the relationship of colors and musical sounds, p. 6090.

I-20. (Book review): Johanne Baptista [Jean-Baptiste] Du Hamel, *De Corpore Animato, Libri quatuor* (Paris, 1673). PT: vol. 8, no. 98 (Nov. 17, 1673), pp. 6151-54.

On hearing; refers to Morland's trumpet and to a similar device by Edme Mariotte, p. 6152.

1674

I-21. (Book review): [Pietro] Mengoli, *Musica Speculativa* (Bologna, 1670). PT: vol. 8, no. 100 (Feb. 9, 1673/4), pp. 6194-7000. [N.B.: Page numbering skips from 6199 to 7000.]
Ref.: LB V-10

Discusses anatomy of the ear, the nature of sound and of hearing; also includes intervals, chords, harmonic proportions, affects, and a discourse on "modern" music. Mentions Birchensha's book, not yet published (see I-16).

I-22. Hevelius, [Johannes].

An Extract of Monsieur Hevelius's Letter . . . concerning the famous Kepler's Manuscripts, together with some considerations of his about the use of Telescopic Sights in Astronomical Observations. PT: vol. 9, no. 102 (April 27, 1674), pp. 27-31, Latin.
Ref.: EL II-67

A listing of the manuscripts left by Kepler, fasc. 7 of which contains items on music (p. 30).

I-23. (Book review): Isbrando de Diemerbroeck, *Anatome Corporis Humani* (Utrecht, 1671). PT: vol. 9, no. 105 (July 20, 1674), pp. 113-20.

Brief mention of the ear's anatomy, p. 120.

1675

I-24. (Book review): Claudii Franc. [Claude-François] Milliet de Chales, *Cursus seu Mundus Mathematicus* (Lyon, 1674). PT: vol. 9, no. 110 (Jan. 25, 1674/5), pp. 229-33.

Lists topics covered in each volume; music on p. 232.

1677

I-25. (Book review): [Francis North], *A Philosophical Essay of Musick* (London, 1677). PT: vol. 12, no. 133 (March 25, 1677), pp. 835-38.

Discusses the nature of sound and elements of music, including harmony and rhythm.

I-26. Wallis, [John].
Letter . . . concerning a new Musical Discovery (dated Oxford, March 14, 1676/7) [read March 22]. PT: vol. 12, no. 134 (April 23, 1677), pp. 839-42.
Original: EL II-44 and II-45
Ref.: JB X-36

Describes phenomena of sympathetic vibrations and nodes in strings, as shown to Wallis by William Noble and Thomas Pigot. Adds observation that a string struck at the node does not emit a distinct sound. (All of II-44 and most of II-45 printed, II-45 being a postscript to the main article.)

1678

I-27. Conyers, John.
> Extract of a Letter . . . of his Improvement of Sir Samuel Moreland's Speaking Trumpet, etc. PT: vol. 12, no. 141 (Sept.-Nov. 1678), pp. 1027-29 (incl. figs.).
> Ref.: JB X-29 through X-31

> Conyers' "Reflecting Trumpet" reduces size of Morland's instrument without loss of power. The trumpet was presented earlier to the Society by Jonathan Goddard and is an improvement on Conyers' 1672 version (see ref.).

1683

I-28. (Book review): John Wallis, ed., Claudius Ptolomaeus, *Harmonicorum Libri Tres* (Oxford, 1682). PT: vol. 13, no. 143 (Jan. 1682/3), pp. 20-21.
> Ref.: PT I-45

> New, corrected Latin translation from the Greek. Topics mentioned, but not discussed, include the nature of sound and Greek theory. Appendix to the book by Wallis discusses contributions of various Greek authors and compares ancient music to "Modern Musick." (For later ed., see ref.)

I-29. (Book review): [Joseph-Guichard] Du Verney, *Traité de l'Organe de l'Ouie* (Paris, 1683). PT: vol. 13, no. 149 (July 10, 1683), pp. 259-64.

> Lengthy report giving many details of Du Verney's research on the structure of the ear; includes information on auricular

diseases.

1684

I-30. [Marsh], Narcissus (Bp. of Ferns and Leighlin).

An introductory Essay to the doctrine of Sounds, containing some proposals for the improvement of Acousticks; As it was presented to the Dublin Society Nov. 12, 1683 [read at R.S. Feb. 27, 1683/4]. PT: vol. 14, no. 156 (Feb. 20, 1683/4), pp. 472-88 + plate.

Manuscript copy: LB V-12

Ref.: EL II-46, JB X-44

The essay is divided into three sections, in all of which the analogy of seeing to hearing is stressed. The first, entitled "Direct Sound," includes discussions of instruments for producing sound, media for transmitting sound, resonating bodies, and improvements to hearing. The second section, "Refracted Sound," deals with air density as it relates to sound, and with instruments designed to convey sound without distortion. The third section, "Reflected Sound," deals with echoes.

I-31. (Book review): Richard Waller, tr., *Essays of natural Experiments made in the Academy del Cimento under the Protection of the most Serene Prince Leopold of Tuscany* [London, 1684]. PT: vol. 14, no. 164 (Oct. 20, 1684), pp. 757-58.

Review of Waller's translation of the *Saggi di naturali esperienze fatte nell'Accademia del Cimento*, originally published in 1667. Among the experiments reviewed are some with sound, including one using an organ pipe in a vacuum.

1685

I-32. Petty, William.

A Miscellaneous Catalogue of Mean, vulgar, cheap and simple Experiments. PT: vol. 15, no. 167 (Jan. 28, 1684/5), pp. 849-53.

A listing of experiments presented to the Dublin Society. Items 55 and 56 deal with sound, pp. 852-53.

1692

I-33. Roberts [= Robartes], Francis.

A Discourse concerning the Musical Notes of the Trumpet, and Trumpet-Marine, and of the defects of the same [read Jan. 20, 1692]. PT: vol. 17, no. 195 (Oct. 19, 1692), pp. 559-63 + plate.

Explains why the 7th, 11th, 13th, and 14th notes of the harmonic series are not in tune.

1693

I-34. Moulin [= Moulen], Allen.

Anatomical Observations in the Heads of Fowl made at several times (read Feb. 1, 1687/8). PT: vol. 17, no. 199 (April 1693), pp. 711-16.

Manuscript copy: RB VI-16

Ref.: EL II-48, CP III-13, RB VI-15, JB X-53

Article largely concerns the anatomy of the organ of hearing in birds. May be the paper described in the Dublin Society minutes (see ref.).

1694

I-35. (Book review): Will[iam] Holder, *A Treatise of the Natural Grounds and Principles of Harmony* (London, 1694) [read Feb. 21, 1693/4]. PT: vol. 18, no. 208 (Feb. 1693/4), pp. 67-76.

Discusses acoustics, proportion in music, consonance and dissonance, intervals, Greek tetrachords, Medieval modes, scales, tuning. (Review by Robert Hooke; see JBC vol. 8, p. 224).

I-35A. Roberts [= Robartes], Francis.
Concerning the Distance of the fixed Stars. PT: vol. 18, no. 209 (March-April 1694), pp. 101-103.

Last paragraph deals with the speed of sound, placing it at 1300 feet per second.

I-36. (Book review): W[illiam] Wotton, *Reflections upon Ancient and Modern Learning* (London, 1694). PT: vol. 18, no. 214 (Nov.-Dec. 1694), pp. 264-75.

Compares ancient and modern music, favoring the modern style (p. 273).

1697

I-37. (Book notice): [John] Wallis, ed., *Porphyrii Commentarius in librum primum Harmonicorum Claudii Ptolemaei, atque Manuelis Bryennii Commentarius in tres libros Harmonicos ejusdem Ptolemaei.* PT: vol. 19, no. 231 (Aug. 1697), p. 668.
Ref.: PT I-45

Announces publication without discussion. (Later issued in J. Wallis, *Opera mathematica*, vol. 3 [1699]; see ref.).

I-38. Hillier, J.

Part of Two Letters . . . dated Cape Corse, Jan. 3, 1687/8 and Apr. 25, 1688. Wrote to the Reverend Dr. Bathurst . . . giving an Account of the Customs of the Inhabitants, the Air, etc. of that Place, together with an Account of the Weather there from Nov. 24, 1686 to the same Day 1687. PT: vol. 19, no. 232 (Sept. 1697), pp. 687-93.

Original: EL II-49 (Jan. 3)

Manuscript copy: LB V-19 (Jan. 3)

Letter of Jan. 3 contains discussion of native customs at Cape Corse (presently Cape Coast, Ghana), including a description of the consecration of drums and trumpets with human blood.

1698

I-39. Wallis, [John].

A Question in Musick lately proposed to Dr. Wallis, concerning the Division of the Monochord, or Section of the Musical Canon: With his Answer to it (dated March 5, 1697/8) [read March 15]. PT: vol. 20, no. 238 (March 1698), pp. 80-84.

Manuscript copy: RB VI-17

Explains that dividing the string of a musical instrument into approximately equal semitones is satisfactory for most purposes, but describes a procedure based on proportions for deriving a more exact tuning in just intonation.

I-40. Wallis, John.

A Letter . . . to Samuel Pepys Esquire, relating to some supposed Imperfections in an Organ (dated Oxford, June 27, 1698) [read July 20]. PT: vol. 20, no. 242 (July 1698), pp. 249-56.

Explains that exact sizes of half and whole steps are possible in vocal and string music, but equal temperament is desirable on the organ, even though this is an alteration of acoustical principles. Discusses Greek tuning theories in support of his argument.

I-41. Wallis, John.

A Letter . . . to Mr. Andrew Fletcher; concerning the strange Effects reported of Musick in Former Times, beyond what is to be found in Later Ages (dated Oxford, Aug. 18, 1698) [read Aug. 31]. PT: vol. 20, no. 243 (Aug. 1698), pp. 297-303.

Original: EL II-51

Manuscript copy: RB VI-18

Addresses the question of whether Greek music moved the passions more than modern music. Surmises that reports of the miraculous effects of ancient music are due to such factors as exaggeration by Greek writers, the simplicity of the ancient people, and the inclusion of acting and verse in musical discussions. The chief aim of modern music is "to please the Ear."

I-42. Lewis, George.

Part of a Letter . . . to the Reverend Dr. Arthur Charlett, and the late Dr. Edward Bernard; concerning some Indian Manuscripts, lately sent to the University of Oxford (dated Fort St. George, [Sept. 6, 1697]). PT: vol. 20, no. 246 (Nov. 1698), pp. 421-24.

Original: EL II-50

Manuscript copy: LB V-20

Describes manuscripts being sent, including one containing hymns in Persian and Hindustani.

I-43. Walker, [Joshua].

Some Experiments and Observations concerning Sounds. PT: vol. 20, no. 247 (Dec. 1698), pp. 433-438 + plate.

Manuscript copy: RB VI-20

Discusses experiments with echoes and addresses question of whether the speed of sound is constant or varies with such factors as wind, temperature, and time of day. (Paper communicated to the Society by W. Musgrave.) Paper may be identical to one read by Walker at the Oxford Society on Feb. 23, 1685/6 (see Gouk, "Music in the . . . Early Royal Society," p. 96, and "Journal of the Proceedings of the Oxford Philosophical Society" in Gun., vol. 4, p. 173).

1699

I-44. (Book review): [Paolo] Boccone, with additional Remarks by Mr. John Ray, *Museo di Fisica & di Esperienze, etc.* [Venice, 1697]. PT: vol. 21, no. 249 (Feb. 1699), pp. 53-63.

Relates common beliefs about music as a cure for tarantula bites and questions veracity of these ideas, pp. 57-58.

I-45. (Book review): John Wallis, *Opera Mathematica*, vol. 3 (Oxford, 1699). PT: vol. 21, no. 254 (July 1699), pp. 259-68.
Ref.: PT I-37

Some musical items, pp. 260, 263-64, 266, and 267. Book contains Ptolemy translated into Latin, Wallis' treatise comparing Greek and "modern" music, Porphyrus' commentary on Ptolemy, *Harmonicks* of Manuel Bryennius with comments, and items on the psalms and on teaching the deaf and dumb to speak.

I-46. Vieussens, Raymond.
Epistola . . . de Organo auditus (dated Montpellier, February 20, 1699). PT: vol. 21, no. 258 (Nov. 1699), pp. 370-97, Latin.
Original: EL II-54
Manuscript copy: LB V-23
Trans.: PT abridg., 5th ed. (1749), vol. 3, pp. 43-57.

Ref.: JB X-59

Anatomical discussion of the ear, including membranes and muscles of the inner ear, the labyrinth, the semi-circular canals, and nerves involved in sound perception.

1702

I-47. Molyneux, Thomas.
A Letter . . . to the Right Reverend St. George [Ashe], Lord Bishop of Clogher in Ireland, containing some Thoughts concerning the Ancient Greek and Roman Lyre, and an Explanation of an obscure Passage in one of Horace's Odes (dated Dublin, Dec. 16, 1701) [read Oct. 21, 1702]. PT: vol. 23, no. 282 (Nov.-Dec. 1702), pp. 1267-78 + plate.
Original: EL II-55

Passage from Horace leads to conclusion that the ancient lyre was made out of a tortoise shell; supported by references to other writers.

1703

I-48. (Book review): [Richard] Mead, *Mechanical Account of Poysons* [London, 1702]. An Abstract . . . sent to the Publisher, by Sam[uel] Morland. PT: vol. 23, no. 283 (Jan.-Feb. 1703), pp. 1320-28.

Offers explanation about why the right kind of music cures tarantula bites, pp. 1322-23.

1704

I-49. (Book review): David Gregory, ed., *Aeuclidis quae supersunt omnia Gr. Lat. ex recensione Davidis Gregorii* (Oxford, 1703). PT: vol. 24, no. 289 (Jan.-Feb. 1704), pp. 1558-60.

Brief reference to two musical tracts, p. 1559.

I-50. (Book review): J[ohn] Harris, *Lexicon Technicum: Or, an Universal English Dictionary of Arts and Sciences, explaining not only the Terms of Art, but the Arts themselves* [London, 1704]. PT: vol. 24, no. 292 (July-Aug. 1704), pp. 1699-1702.

Brief statement on sound, p. 1701.

1705

I-51. Hauksbee, F[rancis].

An Account of an Experiment made at a Meeting of the Royal Society at Gresham College, upon the Propagation of Sound in Condensed Air. Together with a Repetition of the same in the open Field [read March 8, 1703/4]. PT: vol. 24, no. 297 (March 1705), pp. 1902-04.

Original: CP III-19
Ref.: JB X-63

Relates experiment with a bell in a near vacuum, and the effect on its sound as the amount of air is increased. Experiment repeated in open field on June 9. Other, related experiments are reported (but not described) in JB on May 16 and June 13, 1705.

I-52. Hauksbee, Fr[ancis].

An Experiment made at a Meeting of the Royal Society, touching the Diminution of Sound in Air rarefy'd [read March 15, 1703/4]. PT: vol. 24, no. 297 (March 1705), p. 1904.

Original: CP III-20
Ref.: JB X-64

Relates experiment to determine the effect on the sound of a bell when air is gradually withdrawn and then replaced.

I-53. Thornycroft, Edward.
   The Doctrine of Combinations and Alternations, Improv'd and Compleated. PT: vol. 24, no. 299 (May 1705), pp. 1961-70.
   Original: CP III-21

   Mathematical discussion of solving problems involving combinations. Author cites an example from music: how to find the number of tunes of limited characteristics possible on instruments of fixed ranges, pp. 1969-70.

I-54. (Book review): Antonio Maria Valsalva, *De Aure Humana Tractatus* (Bologna, 1704). PT: vol. 24, no. 299 (May 1705), pp. 1978-88.
   Original: CP III-18
   Ref.: EL II-56 and LB V-26

   On the anatomical structure of the ear. (Review by James Douglas.) Printed version omits two paragraphs which appear in the CP; ending section of PT article is not included in the manuscript (last paragraph p. 1985ff).

I-55. Wanley, Humfrey.
   Part of a Letter, written to a Most Reverend Prelate, in answer to one written by his Grace, judging of the Age of MSS. the Style of Learned Authors, Painters, Musicians, etc. (dated London, July 11, 1701). PT: vol. 24, no. 300 (June 1705), pp. 1993-2008.

   Cautions that although an assumption about the provenance or age of a manuscript may be made by its artistic style or handwriting, such assumptions may not be accurate because styles may change or be imitated at a later date. See especially pp. 2004-08 for musical references.

I-56. Salmon, Tho[mas].
   The Theory of Musick reduced to Arithmetical and Geometrical

Proportions [read June 27 and July 3, 1705]. PT: vol. 24, no. 302 (Aug. 1705), 7pp. (Page numbering irregular; consecutive pages numbered 2072, 2069, 2041, 2080, 2076, 2073, 2077.)
> Original: CP III-22
> Ref.: JB X-65

Comments on an experiment performed before the Society in which the frets on a viol were placed at different locations on each string in order to create mathematically pure intervals. Author recommends division of the octave by mathematical proportion, rather than in equal temperament. Fingerboard shown to RS on June 27; performance on viol, July 3 (see ref.).

1707

I-57. Adams, Archibald.
Part of a Letter . . . concerning a Monstrous Calf, and some things observable in the Anatomy of a Human Ear (dated Norwich, Dec. 18, 1706) [read March 12, 1707]. PT: vol. 25, no. 311 (July-Sept. 1707), pp. 2414-15.
> Original: EL II-57
> Manuscript copy: LB V-27

Compares structure of middle ear to man-made drums and makes observation regarding a membrane covering the stirrup, p. 2415.

1708

I-58. Derham, W[illiam].
Experimenta & Observationes de Soni Motu, aliisque ad id attinentibus [read Feb. 18, 1708]. PT: vol. 26, no. 313 (Jan.-Feb. 1708), pp. 2-35, Latin.
> Original: Extra mss. IX-4
> Trans: PT abridg., 3rd ed. (1749), vol. 4, pp. 396-414.

Ref.: JB X-64A

Relates experiments to determine the speed of sound. Shows disagreements among various scientists and presents data which support measurements by Flamsteed and Halley. Concludes that speed of sound is not affected by direction of initial sound, volume of sound, weather conditions (except wind) or type of sounding body.

1709

I-59. Grandi, Guidonis.

Epistola . . . De Natura & Proprietatibus Soni (dated Florence, May 24, 1708) [read April 6, 1709]. PT: vol. 26, no. 319 (Jan.-Feb. 1709), pp. 270-88, Latin.

Original: EL II-58

Manuscript copy: LB V-28

Trans: PT abridg., 3rd ed. (1749), vol. 4, pp. 414-423.

Article seeks to determine physically and mathematically: (1) the paths of sound rays emitted from a vibrating body in a non-uniform medium, and (2) the shape of the sound waves. Also attempts to prove that in a non-uniform medium such as the earth's atmosphere, sound waves will not penetrate beyond a certain plane.

I-60. Hauksbee, Fr[ancis].

An Account of an Experiment, shewing that actual Sound is not to be Transmitted through a Vacuum [read June 1-15, 1709]. PT: vol. 26, no. 321 (May-June 1709), pp. 367-68.

Original: CP III-24

Describes experiment with a bell in a double receiver, the inner one containing air and the outer one having a vacuum. Confirms "that air is the only medium for the propagation of sound."

I-61. Hauksbee, Fr[ancis].

An Account of an Experiment, touching the Propagation of Sound, passing from the Sonorous Body into the common Air, in one Direction only [read June 8, 1709]. PT: vol. 26, no. 321 (May-June 1709), pp. 369-70.

Original: CP III-25

Discusses experiment in which a sounding agent, surrounded by a vacuum except for a small aperture to the open air, communicated its sound through that aperture.

I-62. Hauksbee, Fr[ancis].

An Account of an Experiment touching the Propagation of Sound through Water [read Nov. 2, 1709]. PT: vol. 26, no. 321 (May-June 1709), pp. 371-72.

Original: CP III-26

Confirms that sound can be transmitted through water.

1713

I-63. Taylor, Brook.

De motu Nervi tensi [read Feb. 12, 1713]. PT: vol. 28, no. 337, pp. 26-32, Latin.

Trans.: PT abridg., 3rd ed. (1749), vol. 4, pp. 391-94.

Engl. ed.: R. Bruce Lindsay, *Acoustics: Historical and Philosophical Development* (Stroudsburg, Pa.: Dowden, Hutchinson and Ross, 1972), pp. 96-102.

Solution of two problems: (1) mathematical description of the motion of a vibrating string; (2) derivation of a theory governing the vibration of a string in the fundamental mode in terms of the laws of dynamics.

I-64. Nevill, Francis.

An Account of some ancient Trumpets, and other Pieces of Antiquity, found in the County of Tyrone in Ireland (dated Belturbet, Dec. 29, 1712) [read Jan. 29, 1713]. PT: vol. 28, no. 337, pp. 250 [*recte* 270]-72 + figure.
Ref.: JB X-70

Describes curved trumpets with conical bores found in Ireland.

1716

I-65. Halley, Edm[und].

The Art of Living under Water: Or, a Discourse concerning the Means of furnishing Air at the Bottom of the Sea, in any ordinary Depths. PT: vol. 29, no. 349 (July-Sept. 1716), pp. 492-99.
Ref.: CP III-28, RB VI-23, JB X-75

Portion of article discusses effects of severe water pressure on ear.

1741

I-66. Cleland, Archibald.

A Description of Needles made for Operations on the Eyes, and of some Instruments for the Ears [read Feb. 1, 1738/9]. PT: vol. 41, part 2, no. 461 (Aug.-Dec. 1741), pp. 847-51 + figures.
Manuscript copy: RB VI-28
Ref.: JB X-80

Describes instruments used for curing several types of deafness, pp. 848-51.

1742

I-67. (Book review): Jacobi Theodori [= Jacob Theodore] Klein, *Historiae Piscium Naturalis promovendae Missus primus* (Gdansk, 1740), Or, The first Number of *An Essay towards promoting the Natural History of Fishes* (read Feb. 4, 1741/2). PT: vol. 42, no. 462 (Jan.-Feb. 1741/2), pp. 27-33.

> Original: LP IV-1
> Ref.: EL II-70 and LB V-35

> Describes some small bones which, the author claims, serve as the auditory organ in fish. (Review by John Eames.)

I-68. (Book review): [Claude-Nicolas] Le Cat, *Traité des Sens* (Rouen, 1740; review read Dec. 16, 1742). PT: vol. 42, no. 466 (Nov.-Dec. 1742), pp. 264-69.

> Original: LP IV-2

> On hearing, the nature of sound, and comparison between sound and light, pp. 266-68. (Review by James Parsons.)

I-69. Baster, Job.

> Observationes duae Anatomico-practicae, una de Infante nato cum Sacco Aqua pleno, ab Osse Sacro usque ad Talos propendente; altera de Hydrocephalo singulare (read Dec. 23, 1742). PT: vol. 42, no. 466 (Nov.-Dec. 1742), pp. 277-80, Latin.

> Ref.: LP IV-3

> On bones in ear of child, p. 279.

1743

I-70. (Book review): Colin McLaurin, *A Treatise of Fluxions, in Two Books* [Edinburgh, 1742] (read Jan. 27 and March 10, 1742/3). PT: vol. 42, no. 468 (Jan. 20-Feb. 3, 1742/3), pp. 325-63 and no. 469 (Feb. 3 -April 21, 1743), pp. 403-15.

Reference to "determining the Vibrations of Musical Chords," in no. 469, p. 415.

1744

I-71. Parsons, James.

The Croonian Lectures on Muscular Motion for the Years 1744 and 1745. Lecture II: Containing the Author's Scheme of Muscular Motion (read Feb. 1743/4). PT: vol. 43, supplement, pp. 44-69.

Contains section on the movement of the fingers in playing allegro passages in music, pp. 61-62. (This article is also printed at the end of vol. 44.)

1746

I-72. Southwell, Robert.

A Letter . . . to Mr. Henry Oldenburg, concerning some extraordinary Ecchoes, lately communicated to the Royal Society by the Reverend Henry Miles (dated Kinsaile, Sept. 19, 1661; read June 5, 1746). PT: vol. 44, part 1, no. 480, pp. 219-21.
   Original: BL VIII-1
   Ref.: JB X-86
   Ed.: Old. no. 238

Discusses several "whispering places" and locations with multiple echoes.

I-73. Pepusch, John Christoph[er].

Of the various Genera and Species of Music among the Ancients, with some Observations concerning their Scale; in a Letter . . . to Mr.

Abraham de Moivre (read Nov. 13, 1746). PT: vol. 44, part 1, no. 481 (Oct.-Dec. 1746), pp. 266-74.

Discusses Greek genera, major and minor tones as implied by Greek theorists, and octave division into 31 parts.

1747

I-74. Creed.
A Letter from Mr. John Freke . . . inclosing a Paper of the late Rev. Mr. Creed, concerning a Machine to write down Extempore Voluntaries, or other Pieces of Music (read March 12, 1746/7). PT: vol. 44, pt. 2, no. 483 (March-May 1747), pp. 445-50 + plate.
Ref.: JB X-87

Creed's paper describes a machine which consists of a scroll of paper on a rotating cylinder and pencils attached to the keys of an instrument. As notes are played, the pencils make lines of different height (= pitch) and length (= duration) on the paper. (See Plate 1.)

I-75. Doddridge, [Philip].
Postscript of a Letter from the Rev. Dr. Doddridge . . . to Mr. Henry Baker of one, who had no Ear to Music naturally, singing several Tunes when in a Delirium (dated Northampton, Nov. 3, 1747; read Nov. 12). PT: vol. 44, pt. 2, no. 484 (Oct.-Dec. 1747), p. 596.

Tells of a clergyman's wife who was able to sing while in a delirium, but was unable to do so before or since.

1748

I-76. Watson, W[illia]m.
A Collection of Electrical Experiments. I. An Account of the

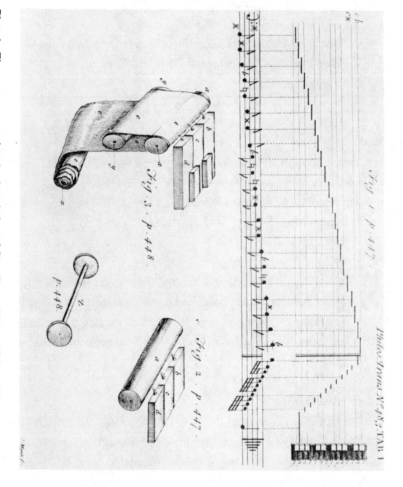

Plate 1. Figure accompanying the description of Creed's machine, which could notate music while it was played on the keyboard, 1747 (item I-74)

Experiments made by several Gentlemen of the Royal Society, in order to discover whether or no the electrical Power, when the Conductors thereof were not supported by Electrics per se would be sensible at great Distances: With an Inquiry concerning the respective Velocities of Electricity and Sound: To which is added an Appendix, containing some further Inquiries into the Nature & Properties of Electricity (read Oct. 29, 1747). PT: vol. 45, no. 485 (Jan. 1747/8), pp. 49-92.

Ref.: PT I-80

Describes experiments comparing the velocities of electricity and sound, pp. 76-85.

I-77. Arderon, William.

Extract of a Letter . . . to Mr. Henry Baker concerning the Hearing of Fish (dated Norwich, Nov. 27, 1747; read Feb. 11, 1747/8). PT: vol. 45, no. 486 (Feb.-March 1748), pp. 149-55.

Ref.: JB X-88

Discusses hearing of fish and propagation of sound in water. Concludes that fish probably do not hear, but have highly developed sight and feeling.

I-78. Brocklesby, Richard.

Upon the Sounds and Hearing of Fishes, by Jac. Theod. Klein . . . or Some Account of a Treatise, intitled, "An Inquiry into the Reasons why the Author of an Epistle concerning the Hearing of Fishes endeavours to prove they are all mute and deaf" (read March 10, 1747/8). PT: vol. 45, no. 486 (Feb.-March 1748), pp. 233-39.

Ref.: JB X-89

Reviews a treatise by Klein which asserts that fish can hear, in spite of an opinion to the contrary by another scientist. Brocklesby strongly supports Klein's view. Also discusses transmission of sound in water.

I-79. Byrom, John.

A Letter . . . to the President [Martin Folkes], containing some Remarks on Mr. Lodwick's Alphabet (read June 30, 1748). PT: vol. 45, no. 488 (June 1748), pp. 401-08.

In commenting on a proposal for a universal alphabet set forth by Francis Lodwick in 1686 (PT vol. 16, no.182, pp. 126-37), author compares vowel sounds to musical notes (p. 403).

I-80. Watson, W[illiam].

An Account of the Experiments made by some Gentlemen of the Royal Society, in order to measure the absolute Velocity of Electricity (read Oct. 27, 1748). PT: vol. 45, no. 489 (Oct.-Nov. 1748), pp. 491-96.

Ref.: PT I-76

Refers to experiments on velocities of electricity and sound reported earlier (see ref.), p. 491.

1749

I-81. Blondeau, [Pierre?].

Remarks on the principal Paintings found in the subterraneous City of Herculaneum, and at present in the Possession of the King of Naples; . . . communicated by Tho[mas] Stack (read Jan. 26, 1748/9). PT: vol. 46, no. 491 (Jan.-March 1749), pp. 14-21.

Describes paintings on stucco in Herculaneum. Five include musical instruments; see pp. 14, 15, 16, 19, and 20.

1751

I-82. Freeman.

An Extract of a Letter . . . to the right honourable the Lady Mary Capel, relating to the Ruins of Herculaneum (dated May 2, 1750; read Feb. 28,

1750[/1]). PT: vol. 47, pp. 131-42.
Original: LP IV-10

Describes frescos, some of which contain musical instruments, pp. 137-38.

I-83. (Book review): Benjamin Franklin, *Experiments and Observations on Electricity* (Philadelphia, 1751; review read June 6, 1751). PT: vol. 47, pp. 202-11.
Original: LP IV-12
Ref.: JB X-90

Brief reference to the effects of electricity on curing deafness, p. 207. (Review by William Watson.)

I-84. Ellis, Henry.
A Letter to the Rev. Dr. [Stephen] Hales . . . (dated Cape Monte Africa, Jan. 7, 1750/51; read June 13, 1751). PT: vol. 47, pp. 211-14.
Original: LP IV-13

Describes experiment with the vibrations of the ship's bell, p. 212.

1754

I-85. Gray, James.
Extract of a Letter . . . to the Right Honourable Sir Thomas Robinson . . . relating to the . . . Discoveries at Herculaneum (dated Naples, Oct. 29, 1754; read Dec. 12). PT: vol. 48, part 2, pp. 825-26.
Original: LP IV-15
Ref.: PT I-86

Reference to Greek treatise on music and poetry.

1755

I-86. Anonymous.

Copy of a Letter from a learned Gentleman of Naples . . . concerning the Books and antient [*sic*] Writings dug out of the Ruins of an Edifice near the Site of the old City of Herculaneum; to Monsignor Cerati, of Pisa, F.R.S. sent to Mr. Baker, F.R.S. and by him communicated; with a Translation by John Locke, Esq; F.R.S. (dated February 25, 1755; read April 17). PT: vol. 49, pt. 1, pp. 112-15.

Italian original + English trans.: LP IV-16
Ref.: JB X-91

Describes discovery of Greek tract on music which blames this art "as pernicious to society, and productive of softness and effeminacy." Tract later found to be by Philodemus; see items I-85 and I-88.

I-87. Wathen, Jonathan.

A Method proposed to restore the Hearing, when injured from an Obstruction of the *Tuba Eustachiana* (read May 29, 1755). PT: vol. 49, pt. 1, pp. 213-22 + plate.

Ref.: JB X-92

Presents case studies testing a method of removing an obstruction from a blocked Eustacian tube.

1756

I-88. Paderni, Camillo.

An Account of the late Discoveries of Antiquities at Herculaneum, etc. in Two Letters . . . to Thomas Hollis, Esq; Translated from the Italian by Robert Watson (dated Naples, June 28, 1755) [read Feb. 19, 1756]. PT: vol. 49, pt. 2, pp. 490-506.

Italian original + English trans.: LP IV-17

Ref.: JB X-93

Describes treatise on music by Philodemus, pp. 504-06. Most of the information on Philodemus is contained in a postscript to Paderni's letter which is written by the translator, R. Watson.

I-89. La Condamine, [Charles-Marie de].
Extract of a Letter . . . to Dr. Maty . . . translated from the French (dated Rome, March 11, 1756; read May 6). PT: vol. 49, pt. 2, pp. 622-24.
Original: LP IV-18

First paragraph describes processing of manuscripts found at Herculaneum; mentions Philodemus' music treatise.

1757

I-90. Paderni, Camillo.
An Account of the late Discoveries of Antiquities at Herculaneum; in an Extract of a Letter . . . to Thomas Hollis . . . (dated Naples, Dec. 16, 1756; read Feb. 10, 1757). PT: vol. 50, pt. 1, pp. 49-50.
Original: LP IV-19

Musical treatise by Philodemus mentioned, p. 49.

I-91. Nixon, John.
An Account of some of the Antiquities discovered at Herculaneum, etc. In a Letter to Thomas Birch . . . (read Feb. 24, 1757). PT: vol. 50, pt. 1, pp. 88-103.
Original: LP IV-20

Describes a painting including a lyre (pp. 98-99).

1760

I-92. Eyles-Stiles, Francis Haskins.

An Explanation of the Modes or Tones in the antient [sic] Graecian Music (read Dec. [13], 1759 and Jan. [24, 31, Feb. 14, 21, April 17, 24, and May 1, 8, and 15], 1760). PT: vol. 51, pt. 2, pp. 695-773 + 3 plates.

> Original: LP IV-21
> Ref.: JB X-95

Lengthy article on Greek modal theory relying on Ptolemy, et al. Clear and extensive coverage of the subject.

1769

I-93. (Book listing): Chatelax [= François-Jean de Chastellux], *Essai sur l'union de la Poésie & de la Musique* [La Haye & Paris, 1765]. PT: vol. 59, p. xix.

Appears among "Presents made to the Royal Society in the year 1769."

1770

I-94. (Book listing): [T.] Jamard, *Recherches sur la théorie de la Musique* [Paris, 1769]; Baniere [= Charles-Louis-Denis Ballière], *Théorie de la Musique* [Paris & Rouen, 1764]. PT: vol. 60, p. xiii.

Items appear among "Presents made to the Royal Society in the year 1770."

I-95. Barrington, Daines.

Account of a very remarkable young Musician. In a Letter . . . to Mathew Maty . . . . [dated King's Bench Walks., Nov. 28, 1769] (read

Feb. 15, 1770). PT: vol. 60, pp. 54-64.
Original: LP IV-25
Ed.: Otto Erich Deutsch, *Mozart, a Documentary Biography,*
(Stanford: Stanford University Press, 1965), pp. 95-101.
Ref.: JB X-98

An eyewitness account of Mozart at age 8, sight-reading and improvising new compositions. Barrington confirms Mozart's birthdate (which he had previously doubted).

I-96. Rose, Alexander.
Extract of Two Letters . . . to Dr. Murdoch (dated Madras, Sept. 20, 1768; read July 5, 1770). PT: vol. 60, pp. 444-50.

Capt. Rose relates his travels to the Cape of Good Hope; article includes report of a coconut shell strung with gut strings like a guitar, p. 445.

I-97. Cirillo, Dominico.
A Letter to Dr. William Watson . . . giving some Account of the Manna Tree, and of the Tarantula (dated London, Feb. 4, 1770; read April 26). PT: vol. 60, pp. 233-38.
Original: LP IV-26

Asserts that music does not cure tarantula bites. Surmises that the theory is a hoax invented for financial gain, pp. 236-38.

1771

I-98. (Book listing): [Pierre-Joseph] Roussier, *Mémoire sur la Musique des Anciens* [Paris, 1770]. PT: vol. 61, pt. 1, p. xv.

Appears among "Presents made to the Royal Society in the year 1771."

1773

I-99. Barrington, Daines.

Experiments and Observations on the Singing of Birds . . . . In a Letter to Mathew Maty (dated Jan. 10, 1773; read April 22, May 6, and May 13). PT vol. 63, pt. 2, pp. 249-91 + plate.
Ref.: JB X-99

An extended essay, in which the author asserts that birds' songs are not innate, but learned. Includes references to instruments and to music in London and in the countryside. Comments on musical elements found in songs of a large variety of different birds, including pitch levels and range, interval sizes and types, scale forms, and dynamic range. Contains musical compositions for "two piping Bullfinches" by Zeidler.

1774

I-100. (Book listing): Charles Burney, *The present State of Music in France and Italy*, 2nd edition [London, 1773], and *The present State of Music in Germany and the Netherlands*, 2 vols. [London, 1773]. PT: vol. 64, pt. 2, p. 495.

Items appear among "Presents made to the Royal Society in the year 1774."

1775

I-101. Steele, Joshua.

Account of a Musical Instrument, which was brought by Captain [Tobias] Fourneaux from the Isle of Amsterdam in the South Seas to London in the Year 1774, and given to the Royal Society . . . . In a Letter to Sir John Pringle (dated Dec. 1, 1774; read Jan. 22 [*recte* Jan. 12], 1775). PT: vol. 65, pt. 1, pp. 67-71.

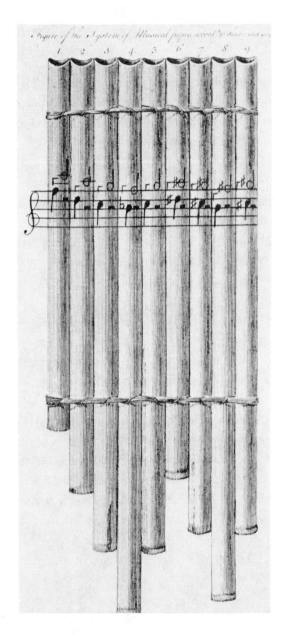

Plate 2. Set of pipes from Tongatabu, brought to the Royal Society by Tobias Forneaux and examined by Joshua Steele, 1775 (item I-101, p. 68)

Original: LP IV-27
Ref.: JB X-100

Describes pitches (lowest tones as well as those obtainable through overblowing) possible on a set of nine pipes brought from the South Seas. (See Plate 2. The island of Amsterdam is today called Tongatabu.)

I-102. Steele, Joshua.

Remarks on a larger System of Reed Pipes from the Isle of Amsterdam, with some Observations on the Nose Flute of Otaheite (dated Feb. 21, 1775; read Feb. 22 [recte Feb 23]). PT: vol. 65, pt. 1, pp. 72-78.

Original: LP IV-27
Ref.: JB X-101

Describes two instruments given to Steele to examine: a set of ten pipes similar to those described in item I-101, and a nose flute from Tahiti (i.e., Otaheite). Possible pitches are notated. Some compositions for nose flute are given.

I-103. (Instrument and book listing): Capt. [Tobias] Furneaux, "A musical Instrument from the Island of Amsterdam in the South Seas" [see I-101]; and John Harrison, *On Clock-work and Music* [= *A description concerning such mechanism as will afford a nice or true mensuration of time; . . . as also an account of the discovery of the scale of musick, London,*] 1775. PT: vol. 65, pt. 2, pp. 546 and 548.

Items appear among "Presents made to the Royal Society in the year 1774."

1776

I-104. (Book listing): Joshua Steele, *An Essay towards establishing the melody and measure of Speech* [London, 1775]; and Charles Burney, [*A*

General] *History of Music*, vol. 1 [London, 1776]. PT vol. 66, pt. 2, pp. 626 and 628.

> Items appear among "Presents made to the Royal Society in 1775."

1777

I-105. (Book listing): [Anton] Bemetzrieder, *Traité de Musique* [Paris, 1776]. PT: vol. 67, pt. 2, p. 860.

> Appears among "Presents made to the Royal Society from Nov. 1776 to June 1777."

1779

I-106. Burney, Charles.
  Account of an Infant Musician (dated Feb. 9, 1779; read Feb. 18). PT: vol. 69, pt. 1, pp. 183-206.
  Original: LP IV-28
  Ref.: JB X-102

> Describes William Crotch, who at age 4 showed a very good ear and an ability to play the organ, but who, unlike Mozart, lacked proper instruction and musical models to follow.

1780

I-107. (Book listing): [Joshua] Steele, *Prosodia Rationalis; or an Essay towards establishing the Melody and Measure of Speech* [2nd ed., London, 1779]; and John Elliot [= Elliott], *Philosophical Observations on the Senses of Vision and Hearing* [London, 1780]. PT: vol. 70, pt. 2, p. 602.

Items appear among "Presents made to the Royal Society from Nov. 1779 to June 1780."

1782

I-108. Hunter, John.

Account of the Organ of Hearing in Fish (read Nov. 14, 1782). PT: vol. 72, pt. 2, pp. 379-83.

Original: LP IV-31

Ref.: JB X-104

Short anatomical discussion of the organ of hearing in fish, with an account of an experiment showing that fish do hear.

I-109. (Book listing): [Alexandre-Théophile] Vandermonde, *Système d'Harmonie applicable à l'Etat actuel de la Musique* [Paris, 1778]; [Anton] Bemetzrieder, *Nouvel essai sur l'Harmonie* [Paris, 1779-80] and *Méthode et Réflexions sur les Leçons de Musique* [Paris, 1781]; and Charles Burney, *A General History of Music*, vol. 2 [London, 1782]. PT: vol. 72, pt. 2, pp. 446, 448, and 449.

Items appear among "Presents made to the Royal Society from Nov. 1781 to July 1782."

1785

I-110. (Book listing): C[harles] Burney, *An Account of the Musical Performances in Commemoration of Handel* (London, 1785). PT: vol. 75, pt. 2, p. 487.

Appears among "Presents made to the Royal Society from August 1784 to June 1785."

1787

I-111. Hunter, John.

Observations on the Structure and Oeconomy of Whales (read June 28, 1787). PT: vol. 77, pt. 2, pp. 371-450 + 8 plates.

Original: LP IV-32

Includes anatomical description of whale's ear, pp. 430-37.

1788

I-112. Jenner, Edward.

Observations on the Natural History of the Cuckoo. In a Letter to John Hunter (read March 13, 1788). PT: vol. 78, pt. 2, pp. 219-37.

Original: LP IV-33

Includes information on the bird's song, pp. 220 and 234.

I-113. Cavallo, Tiberius.

Of the Temperament of those musical Instruments, in which the Tones, Keys, or Frets, are fixed, as in the Harpsichord, Organ, Guitar, etc. [dated Feb. 21, 1788] (read [March 13 and] April 3). PT: vol. 78, pt. 2, pp. 238-54 + plate.

Original: LP IV-34

Ref.: JB X-105

Explains equal temperament, called "equal harmony." Concludes that mean-tone tuning may be used for solo keyboard music, but that equal temperament is needed for accompaniments or for music that modulates frequently.

I-114. (Book listing): L[ouis] Desbout, *Dissertation sur l'effet de la Musique dans les Maladies nerveuses* (St. Petersburg, 1784). PT: vol. 78, pt 2, p. 441.

Appears among "Presents made to the Royal Society from Nov. 1787 to June 1788." (See I-117.)

1789

I-115. (Book listing): Charles Burney, *A General History of Music*, vols. 3 and 4 (London, 1789). PT: vol. 79, pt. 2, p. 318.

Appears among "Presents made to the Royal Society from Nov. 1788 to June 1789."

1796

I-116. Pearson, George.
Observations on some ancient metallic Arms and Utensils; with Experiments to determine their Composition (read [May 26, June 2 and] June 9, 1796). PT: 1796, pt. 2, pp. 395-451 + 5 plates.
Original: LP IV-35
Ref.: JB X-106

Metallurgical analysis of some ancient implements, among which is a *lituus*, an old Roman military trumpet. The instruments were melted down and their composition analyzed experimentally. Pertinent pages include 395-99 and 403-43 + figure 1.

I-117. (Book listing): F[loriano] Caldani, *Osservazioni sulla Membrana del Timpano* (Padova, 1794); and [Louis] Desbout, same title as in I-114. PT: 1796, pt. 2, pp. 508 and 510.

Items appear among "Presents received by the Royal Society from Nov. 1795 to June 1796."

1798

I-118. Wilkins, Charles.

A Catalogue of Sanscrita Manuscripts presented to the Royal Society by Sir William and Lady Jones (read June 28, 1798). PT: 1798, pt. 2, pp. 582-93.

Includes mention of "a treatise on music and dancing," p. 589.

1799

I-119. Wilkins, Charles.

A Catalogue of Oriental Manuscripts presented to the Royal Society by Sir William and Lady Jones [presented June 28, 1798]. PT: 1799, pt. 2, pp. 335-44.

Lists several treatises on Hindu music, p. 340.

1800

I-120. Home, Everard.

The Croonian Lecture. On the Structure and Uses of the Membrana Tympani of the Ear (read Nov. 7 [and 14], 1799). PT: 1800, pt. 1, pp. 1-21.

Original: LP IV-36
Ref.: JB X-107

Anatomical discussion of the muscles associated with the tympanic membrane in man and animals, particularly the elephant. Action of muscles and ear drum compared to monochord; author attributes a "musical ear" to the perfection in the action of these muscles. Includes case studies of persons who lost or gained musical perception resulting from certain illnesses.

I-121. Young, Thomas.

> Outlines of Experiments and Inquiries respecting Sound and Light . . . .
> In a letter to Edward Whitaker Gray (dated Cambridge, July 8, 1799;
> read Jan. 16 [and 23, and Feb. 6], 1800). PT: 1800, pt. 1, pp. 106-50 +
> 5 plates.
>> Original: LP IV-37
>> Ref.: JB X-108

> Some of the topics covered include: analogy of light and sound,
> nature and speed of sound, air pressure in organ pipes, vibrating
> strings, the human voice, and tuning systems. Recommends
> tuning thirds more perfectly in keys with few accidentals than in
> other keys. See especially pp. 130-47.

I-122. Cooper, Astley.

> Observations on the Effects which take place from the Destruction of
> the Membrana Tympani of the Ear . . . . In a Letter to Everard
> Home. . . (read Feb. 6 [and 13], 1800). PT: 1800, pt. 1, pp. 151-58.
>> Original: LP IV-38
>> Ref.: JB X-109

> Relates the case of a man with one tympanic membrane absent
> and the other largely destroyed who was still able to hear, sing,
> and play the flute, his power of hearing being only slightly
> diminished from normal.

I-123. Home, Everard.

> Some additional Remarks, on the Mode of Hearing in Cases where the
> Membrana Tympani has been destroyed [read Feb. 13, 1800]. PT:
> 1800, pt. 1, pp. 159-60.
>> Original: LP IV-39
>> Ref.: PT I-122, JB X-109

> Observation on the preceding article. Home explains that the

phenomenon related there resulted from the sound waves directly affecting the bones in the inner ear.

I-124. Volta, Alexander [= Alessandro].
On the Electricity excited by the mere Contact of conducting Substances of different kinds. In a Letter . . . to the Rt. Hon. Sir Joseph Banks (dated March 20 [and April 2], 1800; read June 26). PT: 1800, pt. 2, pp. 403-31 + plate, French.
Original: LP IV-40
Ref.: JB X-110

Includes paragraph on effects of electricity on hearing (p. 427).

I-125. (Book listing): William Shield, *An Introduction to Harmony* (London, 1800). PT: 1800, pt. 3, p. 732.

Appears among "Presents received by the Royal Society from November 1799 to July 1800."

1801

I-126. Cooper, Astley.
Farther Observations on the Effects which take Place from the Destruction of the Membrana Tympani of the Ear; with an Account of an Operation for the Removal of a particular Species of Deafness . . . . Communicated by Everard Home (read June 25, 1801). PT: 1801, pt. 2, pp. 435-50 + plate.
Original: LP IV-41
Ref.: JB X-111

Having been convinced by further experiments that a hole in the tympanic membrane does not cause deafness, Cooper found that where deafness was caused by a blockage of the Eustacian tube (so that air could not exert pressure on the inside of the membrane), hearing could be restored by making a small hole in the membrane. Several case studies are presented.

1802

I-127. Young, Thomas.
>The Bakerian Lecture. On the Theory of Light and Colours (read Nov. 12 [and 19], 1801). PT: 1802, pt. 1, pp. 12-48 + plate.
>Original: LP IV-42
>Ref.: JB X-112

>Contains numerous comparisons between sound and light.

1805

I-128. Carlisle, Anthony.
>The Physiology of the Stapes, one of the Bones of the Organ of Hearing; deduced from a comparative View of its Structure, and Uses, in different Animals (read April 4, 1805). PT: 1805, pt. 2, pp. 198-210 + plate.
>Original: LP IV-43
>Ref.: JB X-114

>Comparative anatomical description of the stapes in organs of hearing.

1806

I-129. (Book listing): A[ugust] F[riedrich] C[hristopher] Kollmann, *A new Theory of musical Harmony* (London, 1806). PT: 1806, pt. 2, p. 472.

Appears among "Presents to Royal Society in 1806."

II. EARLY LETTERS

(Ms. correspondence up to 1740; archive code EL)

Original correspondence up to 1740 has been preserved in a set of 38 volumes, or "guardbooks," which are classified by letters of the alphabet corresponding to the surnames of the authors.[1] Within each volume, documents are arranged in rough chronological order; however, all letters from a single author are kept together with the earliest letter by that author. The guardbooks contain from about 50 to 150 letters each. Multiple volumes are assigned to a given letter when the amount of correspondence demands it, in which case the volumes are given both alphabetical and numerical designations (e.g., W1, W2, W3, etc.).

The *Early Letters* are in a variety of languages, but primarily English, French, and Latin. Many of the non-English documents written after about 1720 are provided with translations which are inserted after the original letters, thus emphasizing the increasing use of English in the proceedings of the Society. For much of the early correspondence in the collection, a brief summary of the contents is written on the source itself in a later hand.

A catalog of the *Early Letters* was published by W. E. Shuckard in 1840, together with J. O. Halliwell's catalog of the *General Manuscripts*. For each

---

[1] One volume bears a double letter designation: the OB volume contains correspondence between Henry Oldenburg and Robert Boyle.

document, Shuckard lists the writer, addressee, date and place of origin, language, and number of pages -- but not the subject. Many of the *Early Letters* were published in the *Philosophical Transactions;* however, some are unique to this collection, such as those of Carrillo, Cordié, Rameau, and Vieussens.

Archival references below designate volume and item numbers; e.g., V.17 -- volume "V," letter no. 17; O2.35 -- volume "O2," letter no. 35. In this section, spellings of authors' names have been standardized and are given without parenthesis or brackets regardless of what appears on the document. Otherwise, within the entries, material in parenthesis represents that which appears on the source itself; material in brackets is supplied by the editors.

Clean copies of many of the documents may be found in the Society's *Letter Book.* Since these copies often facilitate critical study of the letters, they have also been made part of the current archive (see section V below). An exception has been made in the case of letters to and from Henry Oldenburg, which are printed with translations and editorial remarks in Hall and Hall, *The Correspondence of Henry Oldenburg.* Manuscript copies of these letters thus seemed superfluous for the purposes of this study. In the catalog below, references to *Letter Book* copies, as well as to printed versions of the documents, are cited below each listing; Royal Society references are designated by the numbers assigned to them in the present index.

1661

II-1. Huygens, Christiaan, to Robert Moray. EL: H1.3, La Haye, Aug. 1, 1661
[Julian: July 22] (read Sept. 18), French, 2pp.
Extract copy: LB V-1
Ed.: Huy. no. 881

One paragraph describes his recent work in using algebra to aid
the division of the monochord.

II-2. Huygens, Christiaan, to Robert Moray. EL: H1.7, La Haye, Jan. 4, 1662
[Julian: Dec. 25, 1661; read March 5, 1662], French, 4pp.
Extract copy: LB V-2
Ed.: Huy. no. 953

Portion of letter refers to experiment regarding the sound of a
watch in a vacuum.

1664

II-3. Wallis, John, to Henry Oldenburg. EL: W1.7, Oxford, May 7, 1664 (read
May 18), 3pp.
Ed.: Old. no. 316

Discusses general problem of mathematical tuning of intervals as
opposed to tuning "by ear." This letter, as well as that in item II-4,
presents a response to Birchensha's theories which were
presented to the Society a few weeks earlier (see items X-10 and
X-11).

II-4. Wallis, John, to Henry Oldenburg. EL: W1.8, Oxford, May 14, 1664 (read
May 18), 7pp.
Ed.: Old. no. 318
Ref.: EL II-3

Discusses tuning of musical intervals to create mathematically pure fifths, fourths, and thirds. Relates consonance to mathematical proportions of intervals. Suggests two sizes of whole steps, etc.

II-5. Wallis, John, to Henry Oldenburg. EL: W1.9, Oxford, May 25, 1664, 1p.
  Ed.: Old. no. 320
  Ref.: EL II-4

Wallis has discovered that the calculations he made in the previous letter (II-4) had already been done by others.

II-6. Huygens, Christiaan, to Robert Moray. EL: H1.33, La Haye, August 8, 1664 [Julian: July 29] (read Aug. 17), French, 8pp.; English trans., EL H1.34.
  Extract copy: LB V-4
  Ed.: Huy. no. 1250
  Ref.: JB X-14

One paragraph discusses monochord and temperament. Moray's response to this letter may be found in Huy. no. 1252.

II-7. Oldenburg, Henry, to Robert Boyle. EL: OB.10, London, August 25, 1664, 6pp.
  Ed.: Old. no. 322
  Printed: Boyle works, vol. 6, p. 149

Portion of letter describes a proposed experiment concerning sound vibrations in "hard bodies" (see X-14 through 16).

II-8. Oldenburg, Henry, to Robert Boyle. EL: OB.17, London, October 13, 1664, 4pp.
  Ed.: Old. no. 336
  Printed: Boyle works, vol. 6, p. 159

Ref.: JB X-16

Portion of letter discusses a performance at the October 12 meeting on an Archiviole, an instrument "comprehending both an organ and a concert of 5 or 6 viols in one." The event is not mentioned in the minutes (although Birch adds a footnote about it to his record of the October 12 meeting). Pepys and Evelyn both cite a performance with this instrument at a "musick-meeting" on October 5.

1665

II-9. Beale, John, to Henry Oldenburg. EL: B1.51, January 18, 1664[/5], 4pp.
Ed.: Old. no. 365

Portion of letter discusses theory of how sound moves in air; proposes experiments with echoes and reverberations of strings, bells, etc.

II-10. Oldenburg, Henry, to Robert Boyle. EL: OB.38, London, October 10, 1665, 4pp.
Ed.: Old. no. 430
Printed: Boyle works, vol. 6, p. 199

Portion of letter discusses Kircher's relation of the motion of musical strings to that of pendulums.

1666

II-11. Oldenburg, Henry, to Robert Boyle. EL: OB.50, London, March 17, 1665/6, 4pp.
Ed.: Old. no. 498
Printed: Boyle works, vol. 6, p. 221

Brief reference to musical experiments done in Oxford.

1668

II-12. Oldenburg, Henry, to Robert Boyle. EL: OB.84, London, March 10, 1667/8, 3pp.

> Ed.: Old. no. 808
> Printed: Boyle works, vol. 6, p. 273

Contains a comparison of light and sound reported from France.

II-13. Oldenburg, Henry, to Robert Boyle. EL: OB.85, London, March 17, 1667[/8], 4pp.

> Ed.: Old. no. 813
> Printed: Boyle works, vol. 6, p. 274
> Ref.: EL II-12

Continuation of previous discussion (II-12), comparing the ear's ability to differentiate various pitches with the eye's ability to distinguish intensity of color.

II-14. Wallis, John, to Henry Oldenburg. EL: W1.63, Oxford, September 3, 1668, 1p.

> Ed.: Old. no. 954

Describes an otacousticon, or "ear trumpet," which Wallis had seen 14-16 years previously being used by a partially deaf person to magnify sounds. Includes figure.

1669

II-15. d'Estrehan [d'Estreseau?]. EL: T.33, Caen, May 2, 1669 [Julian: April 22], French, 8pp.

Describes cultural setting of Caen. Mentions instructors of the young in subjects including music and dance. (This document listed in Shuckard catalog under name "Tournes" and filed in the "T" volume. The word "tournes" occurs to the right of the signature and appears to direct the reader to a postscript added on the rear of the last page.)

II-16. Desgabetz, Robert, to Mr. Du May. EL: G1.32, Brolio, September 21, 1669 [Julian: Sept. 11], (read Dec. 2), Latin, 6pp.

Copy: LB V-5

Ref.: JB X-23

Final section of letter discusses a new musical instrument, consisting of a set of strings spanning two octaves, which are brought into contact with a rotating drum by depressing keys.

1670

II-17. Oldenburg, Henry, to Christiaan Huygens. EL: O2.35, London, November 8, 1670, French, 2pp.

Ed. and trans.: Old. no. 1545

Ref.: BL VIII-6, ed. and trans. Old. no. 1542

Reference to an experiment in which a human voice broke a glass. Experiment is described in ref.

1671

II-18. Vernon, Francis, to Henry Oldenburg. EL: V.17, Paris, March 18, 1671 [Julian: March 8], 4pp.

Ed.: Old. no. 1648

Requests description of Morland's trumpet (see I-9).

II-19. Dodington, John, to Henry Oldenburg. EL: D1.22, Venice, May 22, 1671
[Julian: May 12], 1p.
Ed.: Old. no. 1695

Discusses Dr. Cornelio's opinion that tales of tarantula bites are
fictitious.

II-20. Lister, Martin, to Henry Oldenburg. EL: L5.39, York, October 16, 1671,
3pp.
Ed.: Old. no. 1800
Printed: PT I-8

See I-8 for description.

II-21. Lister, Martin, to Henry Oldenburg. EL: L5.40, York, October 28, 1671,
4pp.
Ed.: Old. no. 1808
Ref.: PT I-8

Questions Cornelio's observations regarding tarantula bites.

II-22. Oldenburg, Henry, to Ignace-Gaston Pardies. EL: O2.62, London,
December 18, 1671, French, 4pp.
Ed. and trans.: Old. no. 1844

Relates two acoustical experiments made by Boyle and questions
accuracy of some Florentine observations on sound.

II-23. Oldenburg, Henry, to Philipp Jacob Sachs. EL: O2.63, London,
December 22, 1671, Latin, 3pp.
Ed. and trans.: Old. no. 1845

Describes capabilities of Morland's speaking trumpet (see I-9).

1672

II-24. Pardies, Ignace-Gaston, to Henry Oldenburg. EL: P1.74, Paris, January
13, 1672 [Julian: January 3], French, 8pp.
Ed. and trans.: Old. no. 1859

Contains observations on experiments on sound by Boyle,
Kircher, and Florentines. Also describes plan for a treatise on
motion, including theories of oscillations of strings and
pendulums and the properties of sound and light.

II-25. Cornelio, Thomas, to John Dodington. EL: C1.106, Napoli, January 19,
1672 [Julian: January 9] (read February 8, 1671/2), Italian, 2 pp.
Ed. and trans.: Old. no. 1876a
Ref.: JB X-27

Hypothesizes that symptoms attributed to tarantula bites might
really be caused by heat and dryness of climate.

II-26. Wallis, John, to Henry Oldenburg. EL: W1.136, Oxford, January 18,
1671/2, Latin, 3pp.
Ed. and trans.: Old. no. 1873

Wallis gives observations on Pardies' theories as presented in II-
24.

II-27. Huygens, Christiaan, to Henry Oldenburg. EL: H1.71, Paris, February 13,
1672 [Julian: February 3], French, 6pp.
Ed. and trans.: Old. no. 1886
Ed.: Huy. no. 1866

Presents questions regarding Morland's trumpet (see I-9).

II-28. Oldenburg, Henry, to Thomas Cornelio. EL: O2.71, London, February 9,

1672, Latin, 3pp.
Ed. and trans.: Old. no. 1893

Requests information on tarantula and describes capabilities of Morland's trumpet (see I-9).

II-29. Oldenburg, Henry, to [Nicolas] Toinard. EL: O2.73, London, February 15, 1671/2, French, 3pp.
Ed. and trans.: Old. no. 1900

Describes Morland's trumpet and its capabilites (see I-9).

II-30. Lister, Martin, to Henry Oldenburg. EL: L5.43, York, February 24, 1671[/2], (read Feb. 29), 3pp.
Ed.: Old. no. 1910

Lister comments on Cornelio's theory of tarantula bites.

II-31. Cornelio, Thomas, to John Dodington. EL: C1.107, Napoli, March 5, 1672 [Julian: February 24; read April 24], Italian, 3pp.
Ed. and trans.: Old. no. 1911a
Extract printed: PT I-11

See I-11 for description.

II-32. Vernon, Francis, to Henry Oldenburg. EL: V.23, Paris, March 8, 1672 [Julian: February 27], 2pp.
Ed.: Old. no. 1914
Ref.: EL II-34

Describes speaking trumpet made by Jean Denis in Paris after Morland's specifications. (Denis cited as maker in II-34.)

II-33. Oldenburg, Henry, to René François de Sluse. EL: O2.79, London,

March 4, 1672, Latin, 4pp.
Ed. and trans.: Old. no. 1916

Provides description of Morland's trumpet (see I-9).

II-34. Vernon, Francis, to Henry Oldenburg. EL: V.24, Paris, April 20, 1672
[Julian: April 10], 4pp.
Ed.: Old. no. 1951
Ref.: EL II-32

Notes that the speaking trumpet described in II-32 compares
favorably to one of Morland's.

II-35. Pardies, Ignace-Gaston, to Henry Oldenburg. EL: P1.77, Paris, May 21,
1672 [Julian: May 11], French, 3pp.
Ed. and trans.: Old. no. 1976

Discusses advantage of a hyperbolic shape for a speaking trumpet
and presents mathematical discussion. Includes figures.

II-36. Kircher, Athanasius, to John Dodington, Jr. EL: K.15, Rome, June 29,
1673 [*recte* 1672; Julian: June 19], Italian, 1p.
Copy: LB V-7
Ref.: EL II-37

Extract of a letter (quoted by Dodington in ref.) that describes a
remarkable speaking trumpet in use in Italy.

II-37. Dodington, John, to Henry Oldenburg. EL: D1.29, Venice, July 22, 1672
[Julian: July 12], English and Italian, 2pp.
Ed. and trans.: Old. no. 2023
Ref.: EL II-36

Quotes a letter from Kircher with a description of a remarkable speaking trumpet he ostensibly had invented 24 years previously. Kircher challenges priority of Morland's invention (see I-9).

II-38. Beale, John, to Henry Oldenburg. EL: B1.56, [Yeovil, Somerset?], July 16, 1672, 2pp.
Ed.: Old. no. 2027

Contains observations on tarantula bite and its cure.

II-39. Platt, Thomas, to Henry Oldenburg. EL: P1.82, Florence, August 6, 1672 [Julian: July 27], 12pp.
Ed.: Old. no. 2037
Printed: PT I-13

See I-13 for description.

1673

II-40. Kirkby, Christopher, to Henry Oldenburg. EL: K.11, Dantzig [Gdansk], March 18, 1672/3 [Julian: March 8], 1p.
Ed.: Old. no. 2175

Mentions a speaking trumpet made in Dantzig after Morland's instrument as described in PT I-9.

II-41. Oldenburg, Henry, to Marcello Malpighi. EL: O2.116, London, June 7, 1673, Latin, 3pp.
Ed. and trans.: Old. no. 2244

Brief references to Mengoli's treatise on sound and Birchensha's proposed book.

II-42. Justel, Henri, to Henry Oldenburg. EL: I1.71, [Paris], October 4, 1673 [Julian: Sept. 24], French, 3pp.

Ed. and trans.: Old. no. 2342

Brief references to the Italian manner of singing and Queen [Christina] of Sweden's violin.

1675

II-43. Newton, Isaac, to Henry Oldenburg. EL: N1.49, Cambridge, November 30, 1675, 1p.
 Ed.: New. no. 144

 Discusses [Thomas] Mace's otacousticon as described to Newton by Mace's son. Includes figure.

1677

II-44. Wallis, John, to Henry Oldenburg. EL: W2.36, Oxford, March 14, 1676/7 (read March 22), 2pp.
 Printed: PT I-26
 Ref.: JB X-36

 See I-26 for description.

II-45. Wallis, John, to Henry Oldenburg. EL: W2.37, Oxford, March 27, 1677, 1p.
 Printed: PT I-26

 Most of letter printed as postscript to main PT article. Additions to Wallis' former remarks on sympathetic vibrations (II-44).

1683

II-46. Huntington, Robert, to Robert Plot. EL: H3.72, December 18, 1683 (read Jan. 16, 1683/4), 3pp.

Extract copy: LB V-11
Printed: Bir. X-43
Ref.: PT I-30, LB V-12

Description of sessions of Dublin Society Oct. 15-Dec. 10, 1683. Includes reference to presentations by Narcissus Marsh on the nature of sound and by "Dr. Molin" on the structure of the ear. For Marsh's paper, see PT I-30 and LB V-12.

1685

II-47. Turberville, Daubeney (= Daubigny). EL: T.18, Saxa, Feb. 26, 1684[/5], (read Aug. 10, 1698), 1p.
Copy: LB V-15

First section describes case of a woman cured of deafness by a fall from a horse.

1687

II-48. Smyth, Edward, to the Royal Society. EL: S1.135, Dublin, April 13, 1687 (read July 13), 8 pp.
Ref.: CP III-13 and RB VI-15; PT I-34 and RB VI-16; JB X-51

Cover letter and enclosure of 7pp. of minutes from the Dublin Society from May 24, 1686 to April 11, 1687. Describes a presentation by Dr. [Allen] Moline [= Moulin] on Nov. 15 in which he showed some passages in the ears of birds not previously seen by [Joseph-Guichard] Du Verney. Paper may be that presented to R.S. on Feb. 1, 1687/8 (see I-34 and VI-16).

1688

II-49. Hillyer, J., to Ralph Bathurst. EL: H3.76, Cape Corse, January 3, 1687/8,

4pp.
> Copy: LB V-19
> Extract printed: PT I-38

> See I-38 for description.

1697

II-50. Lewis, George, to Arthur Charlett and Edward Bernard. EL: L6.4, Fort St. George, September 6, 1697, 3pp.
> Copy: LB V-20
> Printed: PT I-42

> See I-42 for description.

1698

II-51. Wallis, John, to Andrew Fletcher. EL: W2.77, Oxford, August 18, 1698 (read Aug. 31), 3pp.
> Printed: PT I-41.
> Copy: RB VI-18

> See I-41 for description.

II-52. Wallis, John, to Hans Sloane. EL: W2.78, Oxford, September 5, 1698 ("post-script, Aug. 27, 1698"), 1p.
> Copy: LB V-21
> Ref.: I-41, RB VI-18

> Postscript to II-51. Letter dated Sept. 5 contains postscript dated Aug. 27.

II-53. Wallis, John, to Hans Sloane. EL: W2.79, Oxford, September 21, 1698 (read Nov. 2), 1p.

Copy: LB V-22

Ref.: I-41, RB VI-18

Refers to errata in II-51.

1699

II-54. Vieussens, Raymond, to the Royal Society. EL: V.38, Montpellier, February 20, 1699 [Julian: Feb. 10], Latin, 12pp.

    Copy: LB V-23

    Printed: PT I-46

    Ref.: JB X-59

Pages out of order in volume. See I-46 for description.

1702

II-55. Molyneux, Thomas, to St. George Ashe (Bp. of Clogher). EL: M1.107 [Dublin, Dec. 16, 1701] (read October 21, 1702), 14pp.

    Printed: PT I-47

Manuscript incomplete and lacking figures. See I-47 for description.

1704

II-56. Valsalva, Antonio Maria, to the Royal Society. EL: V.50, Bologna, September 3, 1704 [Julian: August 23] (read May 16, 1705), Latin, 2pp.

    Copy: LB V-26

    Ref. (review): PT I-54 and CP III-18

Sends copy of his book on the ear.

1706

II-57. Adams, Archibald, to Edward Tyson. EL: A.50, [Norwich], December
   18, 1706 (read March 12, 1706[/7]), 2pp.
   Copy: LB V-27
   Extract printed: PT I-57

   See I-57 for description.

1708

II-58. Grandi, Guido, to Lorenzo Magalotti. EL: G1.74, Florence, May 24, 1708
   [Julian: May 13] (read April 6, 1709), Latin, 16pp.
   Copy: LB V-28 (without figures)
   Printed: PT I-59
   Trans.: PT abrid., 3rd ed., vol. 4, pp. 414-23.

   See I-59 for description.

1712

II-59. Nicholson, Henry, [to the Royal Society]. EL: N1.84, Dublin, October 2,
   1712 (read Nov. 13), 3pp.
   Copy: LB V-29

   Description of a species of birds; includes reference to their
   singing.

1714

II-60. Vieussens, Raymond, to Mr. Manget. EL: V.47, Montpellier, March 15,
   1714 [Julian: March 4] (read Nov. 4), French, 29pp.; summary trans.,
   EL V.48, 16pp.
   Copy: LB V-30, pp. 138-74.

Anatomical discussion of nerves in general, and the optic and auditory nerves in particular. Vieussens endeavors to prove the existence of animal spirits in conveying sensations through the nerves to the brain.

1722

II-61. Roach, Richard, to John Chamberlayne. EL: QR1.60, Bloxham, June 14, 1722 [read Feb. 7, 1722/3], 2pp.
Copy: LB V-31

Proposes improving rhetorical elocution by uniting speech with music, expressing speech in musical notation, and using keyboard accompaniment.

1726

II-62. Du Quet to Isaac Newton. EL: QR1.7 and 1.8 [probable date April 8, 1726 (Julian: March 28)], French, 29pp.
Ed.: New. no. 1487 (QR1.7 only)
Copy: LB V-32

Comprises cover letter (QR1.7, 4pp.) and description of several of his previously completed inventions (QR1.8, 25pp.), including an acoustic device to aid the hard-of-hearing. LB date of Nov. 2, 1721 apparently in error; 1726 date derived from similar document in Bodleian Library (see New. ed. reference for details).

1728

II-63. Carrillo, Joseph Israel, to Dr. Isaac de Segueira Samuda. EL: C2.83, Tunis, August 25, 1728 (read April 30, 1730), Latin, 2pp.; English trans., EL C2.84, 10pp.

Copy: RB VI-26 (Engl.)
Ref.: JB X-77

Describes an African plant, the Verbascum, the flowers of which respond to different types of music. Speculates on cause of this.

1729

II-64. Rutty, William, to John Thomas Woolhouse. EL: R2.14, January 20, 1728/9, 2pp.

Part of letter suggests that Woolhouse thank Rameau for sending his treatise, *Nouveau système de musique théorique.*

1730

II-65. Beighton, Henry, to the Royal Society. EL: B3.17, Warwickshire, March 4, 1730 (read February 25, 1731), 2pp.
Copy: LB V-33
Ref.: RB VI-29, VI-30

Author offers several papers to the Royal Society, two of which concern sound.

1732

II-66. Steigertahl, Johann Georg, to Hans Sloane. EL: S2.33b, Hanover, Jan. 15, 1732 [Julian: Jan. 4], 2pp.

Summary of a letter from Steigertahl which briefly describes a treatise by Sievers [= Sivers, Heinrich Jakob], in which is discussed a stone with musical notation on it.

1733

II-67. Hansch, Michael Gottlieb, to the Royal Society. EL: H4.19, March 21, 1733 [Julian: Mar. 10], Latin, 11pp.; English trans., EL H4.20.
Ref: PT I-22

Regards fate of Kepler's manuscripts; one reference to Ptolemy's *Harmonics* and Hevelius' article in PT (see ref.).

1734

II-68. Cordié, J. de, to the Royal Society. EL: C3.21, 1734, French, 57pp.

(Fifty numbered pages + plates, having some numbering errors; pp. 24-39 deal with music.) Author describes five general substances: "sec, eau, aer, lumière, feu" and five modes in which they occur: "mineral, vegetable, reptile, volatil, genie ou homme." Relates geometrical figures, musical instruments, musical notes, etc., to these substances; compares music with rhetoric, geometry, morals, dance. (See Plate 3.)

1737

II-69. Rameau, Jean-Philippe, to Hans Sloane. EL: R2.51, Paris, August 12, 1737 [Julian: August 1; read Nov. 3], English trans. of original French, 1p.
Copy of original: LB V-34 (French)
Ref.: JB X-79

Informs Sloane that he is sending his treatise on harmonic generation and briefly summarizes the work's content and objectives. Original letter in Brit. Lib., Sloane Ms. 4055, f. 159-159v.

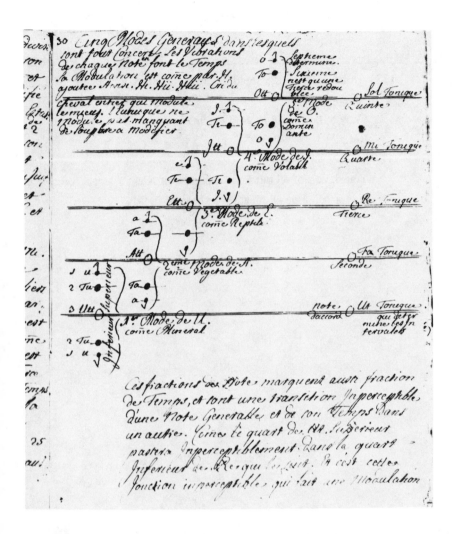

Plate 3. Diagram showing the relationship between the five vowels and the notes of the scale, taken from J. de Cordié's letter to the Royal Society, 1734 (item II-68, p. 30)

1739

II-70. Klein, Jacob Theodore, to Hans Sloane. EL: K.39, Gdansk, October 21, 1739 [Julian: Oct. 10]; [read] Dec. 6, English translation of Latin original, 2pp.

Copy of original: LB V-35 (Latin)

Ref.: PT I-67

Translation of all but first paragraph of Klein's letter. Announces his forthcoming publication on hearing in fish.

III. CLASSIFIED PAPERS

(Ms. papers up to 1740; archive code CP)

The papers submitted to the Society during the same time period as the *Early Letters* (1660-1740) are preserved in 39 volumes arranged primarily by subject. Each volume is provided with a table of contents, which lists author, title, number of pages, and date read. These tables were later copied into a separate manuscript index to the entire collection by A. H. Church. Articles dealing with music are filed in volume II, but additional material may be found in volumes assigned to other topics, such as mathematics or travel, to "book reports," or to collections of the experiments of Hauksbee and Papin. Many of the papers were copied into the Society's *Register Book* (see Section VI below).

Archival references in the following index designate volume and item number: e.g., II.35 = volume II, paper no. 35; VII(1).38 = volume VII(1), paper no. 38. Titles in parentheses in this section are taken from Church's index. As with the *Early Letters*, references to printed and edited versions of the *Classified Papers* are provided when available. For those papers not printed in the *Transactions*, references are given to manuscript copies in the *Register Book*. Undated documents are classified according to the date read, when known; otherwise, they are assigned approximate time periods derived from secondary sources. One item in this section was communicated to Society after the author's death (see item III-29, Robert Hooke's "Curious Dissertation . . . "). It has been listed here under the date on which it was sent to the Society (1726), rather than the date written (ca. 1676).

[after 1642]

III-1. Tasman, Abel Janson [= Jaszoon].
A Short relation out of the Journall of Captain Abel Janson Tasman, upon the discovery of the south Terra incognita. CP: VII(1).38 [journal of 1642-43], 12pp.

> Has brief description of a trumpet-like instrument. (Halley's name as author is inserted in pencil in Church's index and on the cover page of the article.)

1651

III-2. [Aubrey, John].
[A description of] Rainbows, Oyle of Sulphur . . . , Musique [etc.] CP: VII(1).30, London, August 18, 1651, 15pp.

> Includes random thoughts regarding the origin of music and its effects on spirit and health. Aubrey's name derived from table of contents.

1661

III-3. Evelyn, J[ohn]
The History of Arts Illiberall and Mechanick. CP: III(1).1, January 16, 1660[/1], 4pp.

> List of trades includes some musical professions, such as organ-maker, etc., in the category of "Useful and purely Mechaniq." arts.

III-4. Evelyn, [John]
An Exact relation of ye Pico Tenariffe, taken from Mr. Clapham, who had long resided in yt island: as also of severall other particulars

observable there, and written from his owne mouth. CP: VII(1).1 and
VII(1).5 [March 11, 1660/1; read March 13], 9pp.

>Ms. copy: RB VI-1A
>
>Printed (with alterations): Thomas Sprat, *The History of the Royal
>Society* (London, 1667), pp. 200-13.

>CP VII(1).5 is a clean copy of VII(1).1, but with five additional
>pages. Last paragraph of the copy deals with the whistling of the
>natives and how far the sound can carry.

1662

III-5. Charl[e]ton, Walter.

>Apparaty Phono-campticus or What Enquiries are principally to be
>made by such, who would attain to ye certain knowledge of ye nature
>of Eccho's. CP: II.35 (read Sept. 10 [and 17], 1662), 6pp.

>>Copy: RB VI-2

>Relates experiments on velocity of sound. Discusses speed of
>reflected sound as opposed to direct sound and disagreements
>between Mersenne and Kircher. Author describes own
>experiments with single and multiple echoes and proposes
>questions and further experimental ideas. Discusses whether
>length of initial sound is related to distance at which clear echo is
>perceived.

III-6. Powle, Henry.

>Account of ye Whispering place at Gloucester. CP: II.33, October 29,
>1662 ([read] Nov. 5), 4pp. Includes 7 figures.

>>Copy: RB VI-3
>>Printed: Bir. X-3
>>Ref.: CP III-7

>Describes church and its whispering place, comments on some

legends surrounding it and speculates on cause of sounds being carried a great distance.

III-7. [Aubrey, John?]

The Draught and Description of ye Whispering place in Glocester Abbey. CP: VII(1).29, [ca. 1651-62], 1p.

Ref.: CP III-6, JB X-5

Figure of the whispering place described in III-6. Aubrey's name pencilled in table of contents; document appears to be in his hand and is filed with CP VII(1).30, item III-2. The JB reports that Powle's "scheme of [the whispering place] was ordered to be drawn in great . . . which Mr. Winde undertook to do." (See Bir., vol. 1, p. 120, and item X-5). However, this document appears to be different from Winde's drawing. (See Plate 4.)

III-8. Hooke, Robert.

A Brief Account of ye Exp[erimen]ts tryed with Glasse-Balls. CP: XXIV.51 [read Nov. 26, 1662], 4pp.

Ms. copy: RB VI-4

Relates experiments in which glass balls broke under various conditions. Breakage was accompanied by different volumes of noise. Author speculates on cause of breakage and of noise.

III-9. Moray, R[obert].

Account of an Echo. CP: II.34 [read] December 3, 1662, 4pp. Includes figure and musical notation.

Copy: RB VI-5

Printed: Bir. X-6

Describes an experiment at a bay near Glasgow in which a trumpet tune played there was followed by three distinct echoes. Includes figure with map and musical notation of the tune.

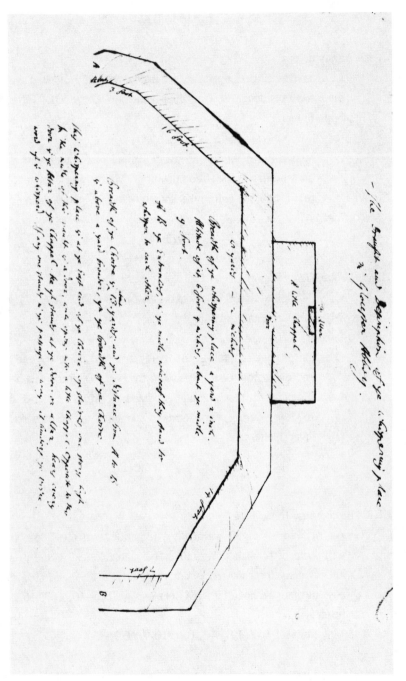

Plate 4. Diagram of the whispering place in Gloucester Abbey (item III-7)

[after 1661]

III-10. Anonymous.

La liste Des Expériences faites dans la Société Royale d'Angleterre durant la Présidence du Chevalier Mourray. CP: XVII.4 [after 1661], 3pp., French.

Lists experiments on acoustics, velocity of sound, and a method for learning musical composition. Moray was president for one year (1660-61) before the Society's formal incorporation.

[ca. 1673-74]

III-11. Croke, George.

Of ye Longitudes; Of ye Speaking Trumpet. CP: XXIV.77 [ca. 1673-74], 3pp., Latin and English.

Third page contains one paragraph on uses of, and desired improvements to, the speaking trumpet. Document is a copy in Oldenburg's hand; though undated, it probably stems from ca. 1673-74, during which time Oldenburg and Croke exchanged several letters.

1676

III-12. Birchensha, John.

An Account of divers particulars, remarkable in my Book; In wch I will write of Musick philosophically, mathematically, and practically, but of many things therein contained, litle or no mention is made by any musical Author. CP: XXII(1).7 (read Feb. 10, 1675[/6]), 3pp. + insert.

Ref.: PT I-16, LB V-3, BP VIII-7, JB X-35

Lists concepts to be covered in a forthcoming book (presumably

"Syntagma musicae" announced in PT I-16). Gives three Tables of Contents covering the philosophical, mathematical, and practical parts of music. The latter two contain many items similar to those in the "Compendious Discourse," BP VIII-7. See ref. for description.

1686-7

III-13. Dublin Society.
The Minutes of the Dublin Society, November 15, 1686-January 24, 1687. CP: XVII.23, 3pp.
Copy: RB VI-15
Ref: EL II-48, PT I-34, RB VI-16

See II-48 for description.

1691

III-14. Halley, Edmund.
(Sound under Water . . .). CP: XXI.31 (read Oct. 7 [*recte* Sept. 30], 1691), 3pp. Includes figure.
Ed.: Hal., pp. 153-54
Ref.: JB X-56

Relates experiments and proposes others to determine whether sound can be transmitted by bodies other than air.

1695

III-15. Anonymous.
Extrait d'une Lettre écrite touchant les Antiquitez de Valoynes en Basse Normandie. CP: XVI.28, Nov. 21, 1695 (read Feb. 19, 1695[/6]), 2pp., French.

Describes discovery of ancient buildings in France, among which is a Roman theater intended for drama, music, and dance.

1699

III-16. (Book review): Hautefeuille, Jean de, *Recueil des Ouvrages de M. De Hautefeuille contenant Plusieurs Decouvertes et inventions nouvelles dans la physique et dans les Mechaniques* [Paris, 1692-1718]. CP: XX.94 ([read] May 31, 1699), 2pp.
Ref.: JB X-60

Review by Robert Hooke. The first part deals with the speaking trumpet. Reviews Hautefeuille's previous work, his theories, and his proposed experiments. Hooke emphasizes Morland's priority of invention and feels that Hautefeuille has contributed very little to the field.

1703

III-17. Wanley, Humphrey.
(Acc[oun]t of a visit to Holland.) CP: XVI.38 [ca. 1703], 4pp.

Discussion of history of printing. Brief reference to printing songs. A condensed version of this paper appears in PT vol. 25 no. 310, pp. 2397-2410, but it omits the reference to songs. (PT article combines CP XVI.37 [also by Wanley on the topic of printing] with XVI.38 into a single article.)

1704-05

III-18. (Book review): [Antonio Maria] Valsalva, *De Aure Humana Tractatus* [Bologna, 1704]. An Abstract of Valsalva's Treatise of the ears. CP: XXII(1).67 (1704), 12pp.
Printed: PT I-54

Ref.: EL II-56

Review by James Douglas. See I-54 for description. Manuscript contains two paragraphs omitted from the PT, but is lacking the last section of the printed article.

III-19. Hauksbee, F[rancis].

An Account of An Experiment made at a Meeting of ye Royal Society at Gresham College May ye 30, 1705 touching ye Propagation of Sound in Condensed Air. Together with a Repetition of ye same in ye open field. CP: XVIII(1).87 [read March 8, 1703/4], 2pp.

Printed: PT I-51.

Ref.: JB X-63

Item no. 87 contains CP III-19 and III-20. See I-51 for description. Date of May 30, 1705 must be an error; JB records no experiments on sound on that day. Paper published in PT in March 1705.

III-20. Hauksbee, Fra[ncis].

An Experiment made at a Meeting of ye Royal Society Touching ye Diminution of Sound in Air Rarefy'd. CP: XVIII(1).87 [read March 15, 1703/4], 1p.

Printed: PT I-52

Ref.: JB X-64

Second paper in item 87; see III-19 and I-52 for description.

III-21. Thornycroft, Edward.

The Doctrine of Combinations & Alternations Improv'd & Compleated. CP: I.7 [1705], 9pp.

Printed: PT I-53

See I-53 for description.

III-22. Salmon, Tho[mas].

The Theory of Musick reduced to Mathematicks. CP: II.30 (read [June 27 and] July 3, 1705), 4pp.

Printed: PT I-56

Ref.: JB X-65

Figures and their explanations are not included. See I-56 for description.

[before 1706]

III-23. Beck, Cave.

An art of memory. CP: XVI.2, n.d., 2pp.

Metaphysical discussion; describes building symbolic "houses" to aid in memory, including a "Brasse Musick House." Article is undated; Beck died in 1706.

1709

III-24. Hauksbee, Fr[ancis].

An Account of An Experiment showing yt Actual Sound is not to be Transmitted Thro A Vacuum. CP: XVIII(1).121 (read June 1-15, 1709), 1p.

Printed: PT I-60

See I-60 for summary. JB for June 1 notes that paper was read and experiment performed; listing for June 15 notes that "An acct of some expts concerning sound" was read.

III-25. Hauksbee, Fra[ncis].

An Account of an Experiment Touching ye Propagation of Sound Passing from ye Sonorous body into ye Common Air in one direction only. CP: XVIII(1).122 [read June 8, 1709], 1p.

Printed: PT I-61

See I-61 for summary.

III-26. Hauksbee, F[rancis].
An Account of An Experiment touching ye Propagation of sound thro Water. CP: XVIII(1).120 [read Nov. 2, 1709], 1p.
Printed: PT I-62

See I-62 for summary.

III-27. Hauksbee, Francis.
The Chief Experiments made this year. CP: XVIII(1).124 (1708-09), 3pp.

Lists several experiments on sound made in June 1709.

1722

III-28. Halley, Edmund.
(Of a Valve near the Drum of the Ear). CP: XXI.41, 2pp. (read Feb. 22, 1721/2), 2pp.
Ed.: Hal., pp. 168-69.
Copy: RB VI-23
Ref.: PT I-65, JB X-75

Hypothesizes a valve in the drum of the ear as a result of reactions of persons submerged in diving bell.

1726

III-29. Hooke, Robert (cover letter by William Derham).
A curious Dissertation concerning the Causes of the Power & Effects of Musick. CP: II.31 [ca. 1676] (read Dec. 14, 1727; sent Jan. 24,

1725/6), 5p. article + 1p. letter from Derham.
Incomplete copy: CP II.32, 6pp.
Ed.: Penelope Gouk, "The Role of Acoustics and Music Theory in the Scientific Work of Robert Hooke," *Annals of Science* 37 (1980): 573-605.
Copy: RB VI-24
Ref.: JB X-76

Gives examples of the power of music to move the passions (e.g., among the Greeks) and cure ailments such as tarantula bites. Explores reasons for this power, including the variety possible with different types of melody, rhythm, dynamics, and harmony, all of which can cause various emotional effects. Hooke also deals with the cause of sound, the ear's reception of sound, the difference between noise and music, and sympathetic vibrations. Article itself is undated; evidence from Hooke's diary and other writings points to 1676 (see ed. cited above). Paper sent to Royal Society by William Derham.

1728

III-30. (Book review): [Jean-Philippe] Rameau, *Nouveau système de musique théorique* (Paris, 1726). A Summary account of a new system of music by M. Rameau, formerly Organist of the Cathedral Church of Clermont in Auvergne. CP: XXII(2).19 (read Jan. 18, 1727[/8]), 8pp.
Copy: RB VI-25
Ed.: Leta Miller, "Rameau and the Royal Society: New Letters and Documents," *Music and Letters* 66, no. 1 (January 1985): 25-26.

Summarizes basic principles in Rameau's new book, which is a "supplement" to *Traité de l'harmonie*. Favorable review by Brook Taylor.

1732

III-31. (Book review): [John Christopher Pepusch with James Lord Paisley?]. *A Treatise on Harmony, Containing the Chief Rules for Composing in 2, 3 and 4 Parts, dedicated to all Lovers of Musick, by an Admirer of this Agreable Science* [2nd ed.], London, 1731. An Account of a Book. . . . CP: XXII(2).53 [read Feb. 17, 1731/2], 8pp. + cover page.
    Copy: RB VI-27
    Ref.: JB X-78

Register book copy identifies Paisley as author; Pepusch not mentioned. According to Hawkins, the first edition of this work was written by Paisley, a long-time student of Pepusch, without the latter's consent. In the second edition, Pepusch apparently added musical examples. See John Hawkins, *A General History of the Science and Practice of Music* (New York: Dover Publications, 1963), vol. 2, p. 885. The favorable review summarizes the book, including: rules of counterpoint, dissonance treatment, cadences, modulation, solfege, modes, fugue, *et al.*

IV. LETTERS AND PAPERS

(Correspondence and papers, 1740-1806; archive code LP)

The *Letters and Papers* form the largest manuscript collection in the Society's archives. They comprise 120 volumes, which subsume the *Early Letters* and the *Classified Papers* for the period 1740-1806. Items are arranged chronologically within the volumes, which are grouped into sets of tens or "decades." (It should be emphasized that a "decade" has no temporal meaning.) Papers are numbered consecutively within each decade. A typed table of contents has been added to the beginning of each volume, citing author, title, and date; as with the *Classified Papers,* these tables have been copied into a large manuscript index of the collection by A. H. Church.

The *Letters and Papers* include a fair number of important documents not published in the *Transactions,* such as two letters by Rameau, Chaulet's work on the voice, and Anthony Gaubil's communication transmitting Chinese songs.

In the present index, archival references indicate decade and paper number (volume numbers are not shown): e.g., II, no. 125 = decade 2, paper no. 125. Titles in parentheses are taken from Church's index.

1742

IV-1. (Book review): Klein, Jacob Theodore, *Historiae Piscium Naturalis promovendae Missus primus* (Gdansk, 1740), or The first Number of *An Essay towards promoting the Natural History of Fishes*. An account of a Book. LP: I, no. 47 [read] February 4, 1741[/2], 8pp.
Printed: PT I-67

Review by John Eames. See I-67 for summary.

IV-2. (Book review): [Claude-Nicolas] Le Cat, *Traité des Sens* [Rouen, 1740]. A short Account of Mons. Le Cat's Book. LP: I, no. 144 ([read] December 16, 1742), 11pp.
Printed: PT I-68

Review by James Parsons. See I-68 for summary.

IV-3. Baster, Job.
(A Letter to Sir Hans Sloane . . . of Certain Anatomical Observations.) LP: I, no. 142 ([read] December 23, 1742), Latin, 3pp.; English trans. of the cover letter, 1p.
Ref: PT I-69, LP IV-4, JB X-83

Cover letter ("exd Dec. 9, 1742") and paper on a "discovery of a process of the malleus, one of the internal Bones of the Ear." According to cover letter, author also sent "two Anatomical Practical observations," but this section appears to be missing from LP. It is printed, however, in PT I-69. See I-69 for summary. Baster's claims of discovery challenged by Nesbitt (see LP and JB refs.).

1743

IV-4. Nesbitt, Robert.

[Letter to John Machin.] LP: I, no. 161 [read] Feb. 17, 1742/3, 1p.
Ref: LP IV-3, JB X-83

Refutes claims by Baster (IV-3) regarding discovery of bones in
the ear. Asserts that these discoveries were already made nearly
100 years previously.

1745

IV-5. Chaulet, Colet de.

An epistolary Dissertation on the Organ of the Voice, in which Mons.
Ferrein's new opinion is examined & attempted to be refuted in favour
of that of Mons. Dodart. LP: I, no. 397, Paris, April 1, 1745 [Julian:
March 21] (presented May 23), French, 4pp.; English translation, 20pp.
Ref.: LP IV-7

Chaulet refutes recent opinions by Antoine Ferrein on the
functioning of the voice, and supports older work by Denis
Dodart. Chaulet not only disagrees with Ferrein's anatomical
descriptions (providing his own, instead), but also debates
Ferrein's analogy between the voice and a stringed instrument.
Dodart's and Ferrein's theories were published in the proceedings
of the Paris Académie Royale des Sciences in 1700, 1706, 1707
(Dodart), and 1741 (Ferrein). For references, see Albert Cohen
and Leta E. Miller, *Music in the Paris Academy of Sciences,
1666-1793*, Detroit Studies in Music Bibliography, 43 (Detroit:
Information Coordinators, 1979), pp. 26-28, 33, 40-43, and 46.

IV-6. [Letter from Henry Baker] to Martin Folkes. LP: I, no. 390, London, May
8, 1745 [read May 9], 3pp.
Ref.: JB X-85

Communicates information from Giuseppe Lorenzo Bruni regarding an eel which died after exposure to loud cello music. Author speculates on effect of sound on people and on animals; includes tale of a dog which had convulsions from the sound of a drum, the medicinal effects of ancient music, the role of music in curing tarantula bites, etc.

IV-7. (Review): Chaulet, Colet de.

An Account of an epistolary Dissertation on the Organ of the Voice: wherein Monsieur Ferrein's new Opinion is examined & attempted to be refuted, in favour of that of Mons. Dodart. LP: I, no. 412 [read July 4, 1745], 6pp.

Ref.: LP IV-5

Review by Thomas Stack. Article summarizes both Dodart's theories on the functioning of the voice as a wind instrument and Ferrein's new work asserting that it acts like a stringed instrument. Author then summarizes Colet de Chaulet's arguments presented in IV-5, which support Dodart's theory.

1750

IV-8. Rameau, J[ean]-Ph[ilippe].

(Of his work on music); a Letter . . . to the Royal Society. LP: II, no. 125, Paris, February 26, 1750 [Julian: Feb. 15] ([read] May 10), French, 4pp.; English trans., 3pp.

Ref.: LP IV-11

Ed.: Leta Miller, "Rameau and the Royal Society: New Letters and Documents," *Music and Letters* 66, no. 1 (January 1985): 27.

Informs Society he is sending his treatise [*Démonstration du*] *principe de l'harmonie* (Paris, 1750), which he briefly describes. According to the JB, May 3, 1750, two treatises were received,

Monsieur

Quoique les personnes qui ont bien voulu se charger, il y a ... 9 mois, de vous faire tenir ma démonstration du principe ... jointe a ma génération harmonique, m'ayent dit que vous l'avies ... Je n'en serai bien convaincu que lorsque vous m'aures ... m'en assurer, soit par votre aprobation, soit par votre critique ... suis trop Jaloux du suffrage de votre Illustre Société, pour n'é... les moyens de l'obtenir.

Si ma Découverte n'a plus tout le mérite qu'elle auroit pû a... dans le tems ou l'on doutoit encore de quelques vérités mathématiques, elle à du moins celui de les confirmer et d'y ajouter, même certaines particularites dont Je ne crois pas qu'on ait Jamais fait mention, par rapport à l'ignorance qui a regné jusqu'à présent dans la Musiq...

monstration du Principe harmonie..p. 19
On voit d'abord dans la Musique, l'unité, un seul corps sonore donner la loy à tout ce qui la compose.

Ibid. p. 20.
On y voit ensuite la proportion harmonique, terme des différens sons qu'occasionne le corps sonore résonant, donner, de son coté, la loi aux autres proportions, et par conséquent à toutes les progressions.

Ibid. p. 21.
Après cela, du frémissement qu'occasionne le corps sonore sur ses multiples, en raison renversée de ses sousmultiples, qui a ... nait la proportion arithmétique.

Ibid. p. 30 jusqu'à 32.
En fin, de l'un des termes de chacune de ces deux proportions, ... rapport à l'inverse avec le corps résonant, se forme la proportion géom...

Plate 5. Letter from Jean-Philippe Rameau to the Royal Society, November 18, 1750 (item IV-11, p. 1)

the *Démonstration* and the *Génération harmonique* (Paris, 1737), both sent by the author. On May 10, Pepusch was asked to review Rameau's work.

IV-9. Ames, [Joseph].
(The ear-bone of the Right Whale shown.) LP: II, no. 157 (read July 5, 1750), 1p.

Describes presentation made by Ames of the "drum bone" of a whale's ear.

IV-10. Freeman.
An Extract of a Letter . . . to the Rt. Honble the Ladye Mary Capel. (Index title: Of Herculaneum). LP: II, no. 109, Naples, May 2, 1750 (read Feb. 28, 1750/1), 11pp.
Printed: PT I-82

Letter dated Sept. 11, 1750 from Wm. Clare, containing extract of May 2nd letter from Freeman. See I-82 for description.

IV-11. Rameau, [Jean-Philippe].
(Of harmonics.) LP: II, no. 84, Paris, November 18, 1750 [Julian: Nov. 7] (read Jan. 10, 1750/1), French, 12pp.
Ref.: LP IV-8
Ed.: Miller, "Rameau and the Royal Society," pp. 28-33 (see item IV-8)

Inquires as to whether the Society has received his *Démonstration du principe de l'harmonie* and seeks review of it. Discusses some of his basic theories including the fundamental bass, the superiority of the interval of the fifth, and problems of tuning. (See Plate 5.)

1751

IV-12. (Book review): Benjamin Franklin, *Experiments & Observations on Electricity* (Philadelphia, [1751]). An account of Mr. Benjamin Franklin's treatise . . . by William Watson. LP: II, no. 212, (read June 6, 1751), 10pp.
Printed: PT I-83
Ref.: JB X-90

See I-83 for description.

IV-13. Ellis, Henry.
Letter, to Dr. [Stephen] Hales. LP: II, no. 214, Cape Monte Africa, January 7, 1750/1 (read June 13, 1751), 2pp.
Printed: PT I-84

See I-84 for description.

IV-14. Gaubil, Antoine.
Extracts of two Letters from Father Gaubil of the Society of Jesus to the late Cromwell Mortimer. (Index title: Of Chinese Music.) LP: II, no. 422, Peking, Oct. 3 and Nov. 6, 1751 (read March 1, 1753), 5pp. + 4pp. music and 6pp. of astronomical observations.

Letters generally do not deal with music but they do inform the Society that some Chinese songs are enclosed. Ten short tunes are appended to the letters (see Plate 6).

1754

IV-15. Gray, James.
Extract of a Letter . . . about antiquities found at Portici addressed to Sir Thos. Robinson. LP: II, no. 542, Naples, October 29, 1754 (read December 12), 2pp.

Plate 6. Three of the ten Chinese songs sent to the Royal Society by Antoine Gaubil, 1751 (item IV-14)

Printed: PT I-85

See I-85 for description.

1755

IV-16. Anonymous.

Copia di Lettera d'un illustre Letterato di Napoli . . . sopra li Codice, o Papiri antichi scavati dalle Rovine d'un Edifizio vicino al Sito dell' antica Citta d'Ercolano. (Index title: Of books and Writings exhumed from Herculanaeum.) LP: III, no. 10, Naples, February 25, 1755 (read April 17), Italian, 4pp.; English translation, 3pp.

Trans. printed: PT I-86

Ref.: JB X-91

See I-86 for description.

IV-17. Paderni, Camillo.

Extract of a letter from Camillo Paderni, keeper of the Museum Herculaneum to Thomas Hollis. (Index title: Of the late Discoveries at Herculaneum.) LP: III, no. 105, Naples, June 28, 1755 (read Feb. 19, 1756), Italian, 14pp.; English trans., 23pp. [*recte* 24].

Trans. printed: PT I-88

Ref.: JB X-93

See I-88 for description.

1756

IV-18. La Condamine, [Charles-Marie] de.

Extract of a Letter . . . to Dr. Maty . . . translated from the French. (Index title: Of papyri from Herculaneum). LP: III, no. 159, Rome, March 11, 1756 (read May 6), 4pp.

Printed: PT I-89

See I-89 for description.

IV-19. Paderni, Camillo.

Acct of the late Discoveries of Antiquities at Herculaneum, in an Extract of a letter . . . to Thomas Hollis. LP: III, no. 215, Naples, December 16, 1756 (read Feb. 10, 1757), 2pp.
Printed: PT I-90

See I-90 for description.

IV-20. Nixon, John.

An Account of some of ye Antiquities discover'd at Herculaneum. In a Letter to Thomas Birch. LP: III, no. 221 (read Feb. 24, 1757), 30pp.
Printed: PT I-91

See I-91 for description.

1759

IV-21. Eyles-Stiles, Francis Haskins.

An Explanation of the Modes or Tones in the Antient Graecian Music. LP: III, no. 413 [read December 1759-May 1760 (see PT I-92 for exact dates)], 66pp. + tables.
Printed: PT I-92
Ref.: JB X-95

See I-92 for description.

1761

IV-22. [Pococke], Richard, Bp. of Ossory.

An account of some Antiquities and curious natural Productions, shown to the Royal Society. LP: IV, no. 39 [read January 22, 1761], 2pp.

Opens with a description of Danish brass trumpets found in Ireland.

1768

IV-23. Court de Gebelin, Antoine.
>Extract of a second Letter . . . to Mr. [James] Hutton. LP: V, no. 28, April 10, 1768 (read April 28), 4pp.
>>Ref.: JB X-96, LP IV-24

>In discussing the similarities among different languages, Gebelin draws comparisons between speech and music, such as between vowels and the scale, consonants and the keys, etc.

IV-24. Court de Gebelin, Antoine.
>Extract of a 3rd Letter . . . to James Hutton. LP: V, no. 67, [Paris], Oct. 7, 1768 (read Jan. 26, 1769), 5pp.
>>Ref.: JB X-97, LP IV-23

>Reference to musical modes, etc., in analyzing sound of various languages.

1769

IV-25. Barrington, Daines.
>Account of a very remarkable young Musician; in a letter . . . to Mathew Maty. LP: V, no. 156, King's Bench Walks., November 28, 1769 (read Feb. 15, 1770), 32pp.
>>Printed: PT I-95
>>Ref.: JB X-98

>See I-95 for description.

1770

IV-26. Cirillo, Domenico.

> A Letter to Dr. William Watson . . . giving some account of the Manna Tree, and of the Tarantula. LP: V, no. 173, London, February 4, 1770 (read April 26), 4pp.
>
> Printed: PT I-97

> See I-97 for description.

1775

IV-27. Steele, Joshua.

> (Of musical instruments from the South Seas.) LP: VI, no. 76, January/February 1775 (read [Jan. 12 and] February 23), 10pp.
>
> Printed: PT I-101 and I-102
> Ref.: JB X-100 and X-101

> Three documents: 1. "The Figure of the System of Musical Pipes (according to their exact size) brought from the Isle of Amsterdam in the South Sea by Capt. Fourneaux to London Anno 1774" (read Jan. 12, 1775), 4pp. (= PT I-101, pp. 69-71); 2. "Remarks on the larger System of Reed pipes, from the Isle of Amsterdam," Feb. 17, 1775 (read Feb. 23), 4pp. (= PT I-102, pp. 74-78); 3. Untitled letter, Feb. 21, 1775, 2pp. (= PT I-102, pp. 72-74). See I-101 and I-102 for description. Printed version includes introductory letter not present in LP.

1779

IV-28. Burney, Charles.

> (Account of an Infant Musician, Wm. Crotch, born at Norwich 5 July 1755; a letter to Wm. Hunter.) LP: VII, no. 91, February 9, 1779 (read Feb. 18), 35pp.

Printed: PT I-106
Ref.: JB X-102

Cover letter and 34p. article. See I-106 for description. Original
letter includes a few passages not printed in PT.

1781

IV-29. Hunter, J[ohn].
[Croonian lecture]: (On Muscular Contraction.) LP: VII, no. 271, June
1781 (read June 14), 24pp.

Includes comparison of muscle with a musical string, pp. 7-8.

IV-30. Guthrie, Mathew.
[Letter.] LP: VII, no. 256, St. Petersburg, Oct. 12, 1781 [read June 6,
1782], 15pp.
Ref.: JB X-103

Describes education of female nobility in Russia; mentions place
of music in curriculum.

1782

IV-31. Hunter, John.
Account of the Organ of hearing of Fish. LP: VIII, no. 3, [read Nov.
14, 1782], 12pp.
Printed: PT I-108
Ref.: JB X-104

See I-108 for description.

1787

IV-32. Hunter, John.

> Observations on the Structure and Oeconomy of Whales. LP: IX, no. 62, May 25, 1787 (read June 28), 118 pp. + cover letter and 8 figures. Printed: PT I-111

> > Includes cover letter from Hunter to Joseph Banks. Pp. 8-17 of section 2 related to sense of hearing in whales. See I-111 for description. (Some rearrangement of material in printed version.)

1788

IV-33. Jenner, Edward.

> Observations on the Natural History of the Cuckoo. In a Letter to John Hunter. LP: IX, no. 80 [read March 13, 1788], 42 pp. + plate. Printed: PT I-112

> > See I-112 for description.

IV-34. Cavallo, Tiberius.

> Of the Temperament of those musical instruments, in which the tones, keys or frets, are fixed, as in the harpsichord, organ, guitar, etc. LP: IX, no. 81, February 21, 1788 (read [March 13 and] April 3), 26pp. + 2 tables.
> > Printed: PT I-113
> > Ref.: JB X-105

> > See I-113 for description.

1796

IV-35. Pearson, George.

> Observations and Experiments on some ancient metallic Arms,

Instruments, and Utensils. LP: XI, no. 1 (read [May 26, June 2, and] June 9, 1796), 82pp.
> Printed: PT I-116
> Ref.: JB X-106

See I-116 for description.

1799

IV-36. Home, Everard.
> The Croonian Lecture 1799: On the Structure of the Membrana Tympani. LP: XI, no. 107 (read Nov. 7 [and 14], 1799), 31pp.
> Printed: PT I-120
> Ref.: JB X-107

See I-120 for description. Includes a few paragraphs not printed in PT.

1800

IV-37. Young, Thomas.
> Outlines of experiments and inquiries respecting sound and light . . . . In a letter to Edward Whitaker Gray. LP: XI, no. 116 (read Jan. 16 [and 23, and Feb. 6], 1800), 55pp. + 5 figures.
> Printed: PT I-121
> Ref.: JB X-108

See I-121 for description.

IV-38. Cooper, Astley.
> Observations on the Effects which take place from the destruction of the Membrana Tympani . . . . Communicated by Everard Home. LP: XI, no. 117 (read Feb. 6 [and 13], 1800), 10pp. + 1p. cover letter.
> Printed: PT I-122

Ref.: JB X-109

Most of article printed in PT. See I-122 for description.

IV-39. Home, Everard.

Some additional remarks on the mode of hearing in cases where the Membrana Tympani has been destroy'd. LP: XI, no. 118 [read Feb. 13, 1800], 2pp.

Printed: PT I-123
Ref.: JB X-109

Appended to IV-38. See I-123 for description.

1800

IV-40. Volta, Alexander [Alessandro].

[Two letters.] LP: XI, no. 137, March 20 and April 2, 1800 [read June 26]; letter 1, 4pp.; letter 2, 15pp.

Printed: PT I-124
Ref.: JB X-110

Letter 1 corresponds to PT, pp. 403-10; last few paragraphs of manuscript not printed. Letter 2 corresponds to pp. 410ff.; first page of manuscript not printed. See I-124 for description.

1801

IV-41. Cooper, Astley.

Farther Observations on the Effects which take place from a destruction of the Membrana Tympani of the Ear; with an account of an operation for the removal of a particular species of Deafness. LP: XI, no. 170 (read June 25, 1801), 41pp. + 1 figure.

Printed: PT I-126
Ref.: JB X-111

Communicated by Everard Home. See I-126 for description.

IV-42. Young, Thomas.
   The Bakerian lecture. On the theory of light and colours. LP: XI, no. 172 (read Nov. 12 [and 19], 1801), 40pp. + figures.
   Printed: PT I-127
   Ref.: JB X-112

   See I-127 for description.

1805

IV-43. Carlisle, Anthony.
   The physiology of the Stapes, one of the Bones of the Organ of hearing; deduced from a comparative view of its structure, and uses, in different Animals. LP: XII, no. 97 (read April 4, 1805), 15pp. + figure.
   Printed: PT I-128
   Ref.: JB X-114

   See I-128 for description.

V. LETTER BOOK

(Copies of Early Letters; archive codes LBO -- Letter Book Original, or LBC -- Letter Book Copy)

A large number, though not all, of the *Early Letters* were copied into a *Letter Book* for preservation. The items were seemingly entered more or less in the order in which they were received, resulting in a roughly chronological arrangement for the 26 volumes that comprise the main portion of this collection. However, five additional volumes form a *Letter Book Supplement*, which contains correspondence omitted from the original set. (The letters in the Supplementary volumes are arranged alphabetically by author, but the collection is not complete.) The Society also authorized a duplicate copy of the *Letter Book*, hence the designations "Letter Book Original" and "Letter Book Copy" (although the original is, of course, in itself a copy!).

While most of the items in the *Letter Book* may be found in the *Early Letters*, there are notable *unica* (such as Birchensha's paper of 1664). It should be noted that the listing below is not meant to be a complete catalog of all musical items in the *Letter Book*. As mentioned in the introduction to Section II, letters to and from Henry Oldenburg are printed, edited, and translated in an authoritative modern edition; for these, manuscript copies seemed superfluous. For other items in the *Early Letters*, *Letter Book* copies are included to facilitate scholarly research, since the copies are generally much more readable than the originals.

The Society's archives house a hand-written subject index to the *Letter Book, Register Book,* and *Journal Book,* but it covers items only up to 1695. In the following catalog, archival references designate LBC or LBO, volume, and page numbers; e.g. LBC: 12.3-5 = Letter Book Copy, vol. 12, pp. 3-5.

1661

V-1. Huygens, [Christiaan].

An Extract of a Letter . . . To Sr. R. Moray Touching The Application of Algebra to Musick. LBC: 1.57-8, La Haye, August 1, 1661 [Julian: July 22; read Sept. 18], French.

Original: EL II-1

Ed.: Huy. no. 881

Only one paragraph of letter copied in LB (on monochord). See II-1 for description. (See Plate 7.)

V-2. Huygens, [Christiaan].

Extract of a letter . . . to Sr. R. Moray Concerning some Exp[erimen]ts made in the Pneumatick Engine. LBO: 1.26-27, La Haye, January 4, 1662 [Julian: Dec. 25, 1661; read March 8, 1662], French.

Original: EL II-2

Ed.: Huy. no. 953

Most of letter copied with the exception of a few opening sentences. See II-2 for description.

1664

V-3. Birshensha, [John].

An Extract of A Letter Written to the Royall Society . . . Concerning Musick. LBC: 1.166-73, April 26, 1664 [read April 27].

Ref.: BP VIII-7, PT I-16, CP III-12, JB X-11

Birchensha sets forth the contents of a proposed treatise, including the principles of the mathematical part of music, a perfect scale, and rules by which anyone could learn to compose in a few weeks. Instructions on how to write counterpoint, fugue, and canons would also be provided. The treatise is presumably

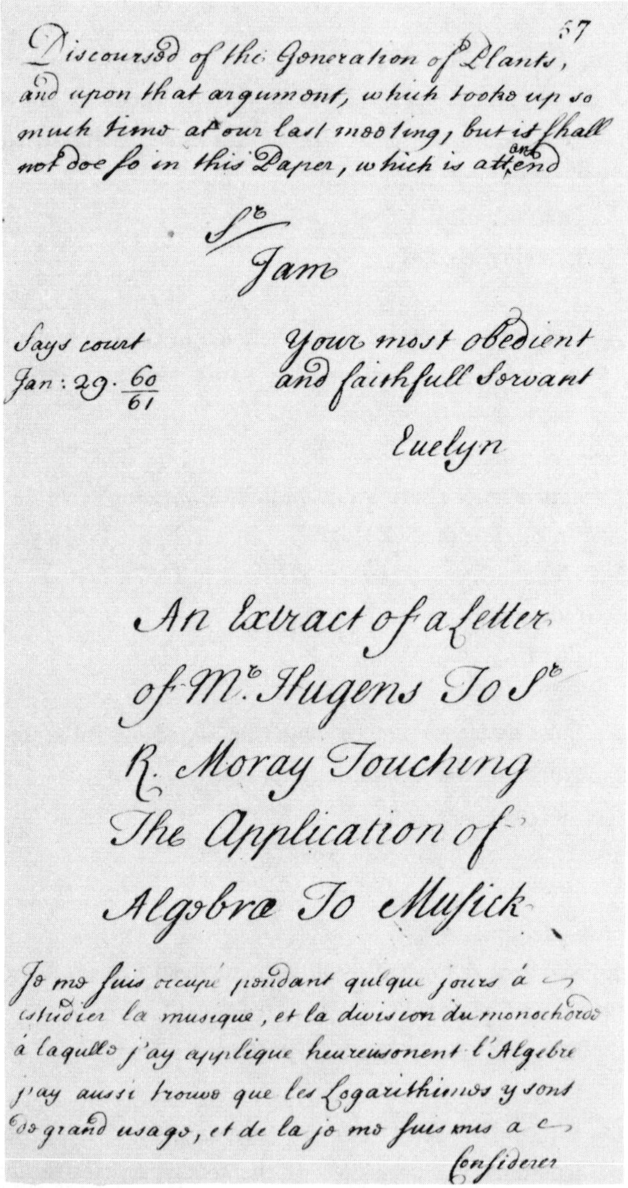

57

Discoursed of the Generation of Plants, and upon that argument, which tooke up so much time at our last meeting; but it shall not doe so in this Paper, which is attend

Sr

I am

Says court
Jan: 29. 60/61

Your most obedient
and faithfull Servant

Euelyn

An Extract of a letter
of Mr. Hugens To Sr
R. Moray Touching
The Application of
Algebra To Musick

Je me suis occupé pendant quelque jours à estudier la musique, et la division du monochorde à laquelle j'ay appliqué heureusement l'Algebre j'ay aussi trouvé que les logarithmes y sont de grand usage, et de la je me suis mis a considerer

Plate 7. Copy of a letter from Christiaan Huygens to the Royal Society, 1661 (item V-1, p. 57)

related to his "Compendious Discourse" (item VIII-7) and the work described in I-16 and III-12.

V-4. Huygens, [Christiaan].

An Extract of a Letter . . . to Sr. Robert Moray, Concerning [a new pendulum] watch, Experiments of Musicall Chordes, Compression of Air, Magnet with 4 Poles. Dr. Wallis booke de Cerebri Anatome, New Charret, and a Telescope of Sixty foot. LBC: 1.206-11, La Haye, August 8, 1664 [Julian: July 29; read Aug. 17], French.

Original: EL II-6
Ed.: Huy. no. 1250
Ref.: JB X-14

Most of letter copied. See II-6 for description.

1669

V-5. Desgabetz, Robert.

A Letter . . . to Mr. Du May concerning the Copernican System of the World; perpetual Motion; the Application of a Pendulum to a Pocket Watch, a new Mill: and Improvements in Navigation and Musick by new Instruments. LBO Supp.: 4.1-13, Brolio, September 21, 1669 [Julian: Sept. 11] (read Dec. 2), Latin.

Original: EL II-16
Ref.: JB X-23

See II-16 for description.

1671

V-6. Pardies, Ignace-Gaston.

Abstract of a Letter of the Jesuit Pardies to Mr. Oldenb[urg], speaking of the high esteem he hath of the Philosophicall men & Books of England, as also of the Florentine Experiment about Sounds in vacuo,

together with his design of printing a Book about motion. LBC: 5.25-27, Paris, Oct. 20, 1671 [Julian: Oct. 10; read Dec. 14], French.
>   Ed.: Old. no. 1794
>   Ref.: JB X-26

>   Pardies expresses doubt about a Florentine experiment which showed that sound can be propagated in a vacuum.

1672

V-7. Kircher, [Athanasius].
>   Extract of a Letter . . . to Mr. Dodington junior, concerning a remarkable Speaking Trumpet. LBO Supp.: 5.290, Rome, June 29, 1673 [*recte*, 1672; Julian: June 19], Italian.
>   Original: EL II-36
>   Ref.: EL II-37

>   See II-36 for description.

1683

V-8. Plot, [Robert].
>   Some Experiments sent from Oxford. LBC: 8.398-402, February 12, 1682[/3], [read Feb. 14].
>   Printed: Bir. X-41

>   Contains section on curing deafness through exposure to loud bells, pp. 401-02.

V-9. Mariotte, [Edme].
>   [A letter] to Mr. Aston About Shortening of Pendules; Observations with the Barometer and pendules . . . . Mr. Verney of the organs of hearing & his owne Hypothesis & of Vision. LBC: 8.487-90, Paris, April 25, 1683 [Julian: April 15; read May 16], French.

Ref.: JB X-42

Comments on Du Verney's treatise on the ear, and presents Mariotte's own hypothesis on nerves involved in vision and hearing, pp. 488-89.

V-10. Musgrave, [William]

[A letter] to Mr. Aston about the Magnet and Magnatism [*sic*], Dr. Wallis chimney Piece with minerall Figures, about Hearing and the Earthquake. LBC: 9.53-55, Oxford, November 3, 1683.

Refers to a Dr. Aldrege (or Aldrich) in Oxford, who hypothesized that there must be two drums in the ear, and to Mengoli's treatise (see PT I-21), p. 54. Aldrich's presentation to the Oxford Society took place on Nov. 2, 1683 (see Oxford Society Minutes in Gun., vol. 4, p. 20).

V-11. Huntington, Rob[er]t.

An Abstract of a Letter . . . to Dr. Plot about the Meeting at Dublin. LBC: 9.131-8, December 18, 1683 [read Jan. 16, 1683/4].

Original: EL II-46
Printed: Bir. X-43
Ref.: PT I-30, LB V-12

Most of letter presented, but order of material rearranged. See II-46 for description. This item is followed immediately by copy of Marsh's paper, V-12.

V-12. [Marsh], Narcissus.

An Introductory Essay to the Doctrine of Sounds Containing some Proposalls for the Improvement of Acoustick. As it was presented to the Dublin Society Novemb[er] 12, 1683. LBC: 9.138-164 [read at RS Feb. 27, 1683/4].

Printed: PT I-30

Ref.: JB X-44

See I-30 for description.

1684

V-13. Molyneux, William.

Mr. Molyneux to Mr. Aston with the Minutes of the Dublin Society for A Month from February the 10th to March the 10th 1683/4. LBO: 9.143-48, March 15, 1683/4 [read March 26].
Printed: Bir. X-45

Cover letter (pp. 147-48) and minutes of Dublin Society (pp. 143-47), including presentations by Dr. Mullen [*sic*] on Feb. 25 and March 3 regarding anatomical discoveries in ears of calf and pullet.

V-14. Davis, John.

[A letter] to Mr. Aston about his Engine for weaving, Contrivance about musicall Instruments . . . etc. LBC: 9.213-214, Nottinghamshire, April 5, 1684 [read April 23].

Author has found a way of "contriving" several sorts of musical instruments so that any tune may be played on them.

1685

V-15. Turbervile, Dawleney [= Daubeney or Daubigny].

A Letter . . . concerning Several Cures. LBC: 12.3-5, Saxa, Feb. 26, 1684[/5], [read Aug. 10, 1698].
Original: EL II-47

See II-47 for description.

V-16. Musgrave, [William].

    [A letter] . . . to Mr. Aston with the Suppellex Philosophica of Sr. Wm. Petty. A Tobacco pipe in the Bladder, of Mr. Colbrons Cutting out a Stone after Dr. Listers way. LBC: 10.175-77, May 1, 1685 [read May 6].

    Excerpt printed: Bir. X-49

    Gives listing of scientific instruments, which includes monochord, speaking trumpet, and acoustic tube (see Bir. ref.).

V-17. Justel, [Henri].

    [A letter] . . . to Mr. Aston about A Secret of making two persons of different Languages understand one another in 1/4 of an hour: That ye Machine for goeing under water is finished: Of a Peare found Sound after 100 years being under ground: A new sort of Organ . . . [etc.]. LBC: 10.255-7 [ca. 1685], French.

    Describes new organ by M. Perrot [= Claude Perrault] which has diverse stops and is operated by a foot pedal. Promises a more detailed description.

1686

V-18. Ash[e], St. George.

    [A letter] . . . to [the] Royal Society. LBC: 10.365-6, Dublin, March 13, 1685/6 (read March 24).

    Brief letter relating presentations at Dublin Society, among which was a case of an 11-year old girl skillful in all subjects including "speculative musick."

1688

V-19. Hillyer, J.

A Letter . . . to Dr. Bathurst, giving an account of the Climate of Cape Corse, with the Manners & Customs of the Inhabitants. LBO Supp.: 4.413-22, Cape Corse, January 3, 1687/8.

> Extract printed: PT I-38
> Original: EL II-49

> See I-38 for description.

1697

V-20. Lewis, George.

Letter from Fort St. George Communicated to the Royal Society by Dr. Arthur Charlett. LBC: 11(2).67a-69, September 6, 1697.

> Printed: PT I-42
> Original: EL II-50

> See I-42 for description.

1698

V-21. Wallis, John.

A Letter . . . to Dr. Sloane Concerning his Musicall Observations and Instructions. LBC: 11(2).311-12, Oxford, September 5, 1698.

> Original: EL II-52
> Ref.: PT I-41, RB VI-18

> See II-52 for description.

V-22. Wallis, John.

A Letter . . . to Dr. Sloane concerning the Veering of the Trade Wind at Barbadoes. LBC: 11(2).314-6, Oxford, September 21, 1698 [read Nov.

2].

> Original: EL II-53.
> Ref.: PT I-41, RB VI-18

> See II-53 for description.

1699

V-23. Vieussens, [Raymond].

> Epistola . . . De Organo Auditus. LBC: 12.186-91 [Montpellier, February 20; Julian: Feb. 10], 1699, Latin.
> Printed: PT I-46
> Original: EL II-54
> Ref.: JB X-59

> See I-46 for description.

V-24. Herbert, John.

> A Letter . . . To the Royall Society. LBC: 12.372-4, Montpellier, Feb. 22, 1699 [Julian: Feb. 12].
> Ref.: LB V-23

> Herbert encloses Vieussens' work on the ear (V-23), which contains theories contrary to those of Du Verney. Author warns Royal Society to review the work carefully, so as not to be caught in a "French quarrel."

V-25. Sloane, [Hans].

> A Letter . . . to Mr. Vieussens. LBC: 12.101-2, March 24, 1699, Latin.

> Thanks Vieussens for his communication to the Royal Society regarding the ear.

1704

V-26. Valsalva, Antonio Maria.

Epistola . . . De Tractatu suo de Aure Humana. LBC: 14.67-8, Bologna, September 3, 1704 [Julian: August 23; read May 16, 1705], Latin.

Original: EL II-56
Ref. (review): CP III-18 and PT I-54

See II-56 for description.

1706

V-27. Adams, Archibald.

A Letter . . . to Dr. Tyson, containing an account of a monstrous Calf, an observation and Description of the Drum of the Human Ear, and offering to make a Present to the R. Society of his Preparation of the Ear. LBO Supp.: 1.128-31, Norwich, Dec. 18, 1706 (read March 12, 1706[/7]).

Extract printed: PT I-57
Original: EL II-57

See I-57 for description.

1708

V-28. Grandi, Guido.

A Letter . . . to Count Magalotti, concerning the Nature and Properties of Sound. LBO Supp.: 4.66-88, Florence, May 24, 1708 [Julian: May 13] (read April 6, 1709), Latin.

Original: EL II-58
Printed: PT I-59

Copy lacks figures. See I-59 for description.

1712

V-29. Nicholson, Henry.

An Account of the Loxia or Curvi Rostra. LBC: 16.4-7, Dublin, October 2, 1712 [read Nov. 13].

Original: EL II-59

See II-59 for description.

1714

V-30. Vieussens, [Raymond].

[Three letters]. LBC: 16.136-74, March [15 and] 20, 1714 [Julian: March 4 and 9] (read Nov. 4), one in Latin, two in French.

Original and summary trans. of third letter: EL II-60.

See II-60 for description.

1722

V-31. Roach, R[ichar]d.

A Letter . . . to John Chamberlayne Esq. about Rhetorical Elocution. LBC: 16.323-5, Bloxham, June 14, 1722 (read Feb. 7, 1722[/3]).

Original: EL II-61

See II-61 for description.

1726

V-32. Du Quet.

A Letter . . . to Sir Is: Newton: of his having found the Longitude, [and] Extrait des Memoires presentez a la Cour. LBC: 15.379-80 and 381-89, Paris [April 8. 1726?; Julian: March 28], French.

Original: EL II-62

Ed.: New. no. 1487 (letter only)

Date read of Nov. 2, 1721, which appears on this document, is apparently an error (see ed. ref.). See II-62 for description.

1730

V-33. Beighton, H[enry].
[Letter] to the Royal Society. LBC: 19.350-2, Warwickshire, March 4, 1730 [read Feb. 25, 1731].
Original: EL II-65

See II-65 for description.

1737

V-34. Rameau, [Jean-Philippe].
A Letter . . . to the President [Hans Sloane], accompanying the Present of his Book of Musick made to the Royal Society. LBC: 24.24-5, Paris, August 12, 1737 [Julian: August 1] (trans. read Nov. 3, 1737), French.
Trans. of original: EL II-69
Ref.: JB X-79

Copy of French original. See II-69 for description.

1739

V-35. Klein, [Jacob Theodore].
A Letter . . . to the President [Hans Sloane], giving Notice of his first Essay on the natural History of Fishes now in the Press and recommending Dr. de Superville for Election into the Society. LBC: 26.436-7, Gdansk, October 21, 1739 [Julian: October 10] (trans. read Dec. 6, 1739), Latin.

Trans. of original: EL II-70
Ref.: PT I-67

Copy of Latin original. See II-70 for description.

VI. REGISTER BOOK

(Copies of Classified Papers and other materials,
1660-1740; archive codes RBO -- Register Book Original, or
RBC -- Register Book Copy)

Important papers read at Royal Society meetings up to 1740 were often ordered to be entered in the *Register Book;* the originals of many of these are now found in the *Classified Papers.* The 21 volumes that comprise the *Register Book,* like those of the *Letter Book,* exist in duplicate in the archives.[1] The *Register Book Copy,* however, is sometimes less reliable and less legible than the original. References in the present index are to the more reliable texts, whether in the RBO or the RBC.

It should be noted that volume 10 is missing from the set. It was apparently already gone ca. 1740, since cross references to specific pages in it are lacking in Martin Folkes' index of the *Journal Book* compiled about that date.[2] There is no complete index to the *Register Book;* a manuscript subject index exists, but it covers only the period up to 1695 (see above, in the introduction to section V).

---

[1] Curiously, there are three copies of volume 2, two of them in the RBO series.

[2] Folkes must have known some of the items which were entered in volume 10 from his examination of the minutes. For these items, he notes "vol. 10," but provides no page numbers.

Archival references in the present catalog designate RBO or RBC, with volume and page numbers; e.g., RBO: 2.52-54 = Register Book Original, volume 2, pp. 52-54. For items in the *Classified Papers* that were printed in the *Transactions,* no *Register Book* copies are listed here.

Items are filed under the date that appears in the *Register Book* (usually the date read). In most cases, this date is within a few months of the date written. Exceptions are: (1) Hooke's paper on the effects of music (VI-24; see CP III-29 for discussion), and (2) the papers of Henry Beighton, which were sent to the Society some years after the experiments were performed (see VI-29).

1661

VI-1. Brouncker, William, and Robert Boyle.

> Questions Propounded by Ld. Brounker and Mr. Boyle, And agreed uppon to be sent to Tenariff. RBO: 1.1-2 [read] Jan. 2, 1660/1.
>
> Printed: Bir. X-1

> List of questions to investigate; no. 16 on sound.

VI-1A. Evelyn, John.

> An Exact Relation of the Pico Tenariff taken from Mr. Clappham. RBC: 1.43-56 [March 11, 1660/1; read March 13].
>
> Original: CP III-4

> See III-4 for description.

1662

VI-2. Charl[e]ton, [Walter].

> Dr. Charlton's Apparatus Phonocampticus or What Enquiries are principally to be made by such who would attain to the certain knowledge of the Nature of Eccho's. RBO: 1.197-205 [read Sept. 10 and 17, 1662].
>
> Original: CP III-5

> See III-5 for description.

VI-3. Powle, Henry.

> Account of the Whispering-place at Gloucester. RBO: 2.31-36, October 29, 1662 [read Nov. 5].
>
> Original: CP III-6
> Printed: Bir. X-3

> See III-6 for description.

VI-4. Hook[e], [Robert].
A Breif [*sic*] Account of the Experiments try'd with Glasse Balls. RBO: 2.37-41, [read] November 26, 1662.
Original: CP III-8

See III-8 for description.

VI-5. Moray, Robert.
An Account of an Echo. RBO: 2.52-54, [read] December 3, 1662.
Original: CP III-9
Printed: Bir. X-6

See III-9 for description.

1663

VI-6. Brouncker, William, Robert Moray, Alexander Bruce, Robert Hooke.
An Account of the Experiments and Observations made . . . upon the Thames. RBO: 2.208-13, read March 18, 1662[/3].
Printed: Bir. X-8

Includes "Observations of Sound," related to echoes caused by gun fire on the Thames (p. 213).

1668

VI-7. Hook[e], [Robert].
The Description of An Instrument for collecting the Wind Or, for making the slower motions of the Air more sensible. RBO: 3.294-5, March 12, 1667/8 [read March 19].
Printed: Bir. X-18

Describes an instrument for collecting wind (including a figure), and adds that a similar one could be used for collecting and augmenting sounds, thus aiding the hard of hearing.

VI-8. Holder, [William].

A Breif [*sic*] Account of An Experiment concerning Deafnesse. RBO: 3.301-3, read April 23, 1668.

Printed: PT I-3

See I-3 for description.

1672

VI-9. Hooke, Robert.

Considerations of Mr. Hook[e] upon Mr. Newton's Discourse of Light and Colours. RBO: 4.148-54 [read Feb. 15, 1671/2].

Printed: Bir. X-28

Includes comparison of sound and light.

1674

VI-10. Petty, William.

A Discourse [on duplicate and subduplicate proportions] to the Royall Society. RBO: 4.246-267, read November 26, 1674.

Ref.: JB X-32

Discusses various uses of duplicate and subduplicate proportions. Item 7 concerns sound -- how far a gun shot may be heard in relation to the number of guns producing the shot. Item 12 deals with music -- variation in pitch resulting from change in tension on a string. *Discourse* published: London, 1674.

1675

VI-11. Newton, Isaac.

Mr. Isaac Newton's Letter, Hypothesis, Observations and Experiments, touching his Theory of Light and Colors, in confirmation and Illustration of his former discourse on the same subject. RBO: 5.65-124 [Cambridge, Dec. 7, 1675], read Dec. 9.

    Printed: Bir. X-34

    Ed.: New., nos. 145 and 146

    Comparisons of sound and light included in discussion of colors.

1684

VI-12. Papin, [Denis].

About the Florentine Experiments, etc. RBC: 6.154-6, [read] November 26, 1684.

    Printed: Bir. X-46

    One item deals with sound production in a vacuum. Papin concludes that the Florentine apparatus was faulty, and that air is necessary for sound.

1685

VI-13. Papin, [Denis].

Experiment to prove that the Air is Necessary for Sounds. RBC: 6.166, [read] March 11, 1684/5.

    Printed: Bir. X-47

    Describes experiment with a pipe in a receiver through which air is pumped. Concludes that air is necessary for sound. (See Plate 8.)

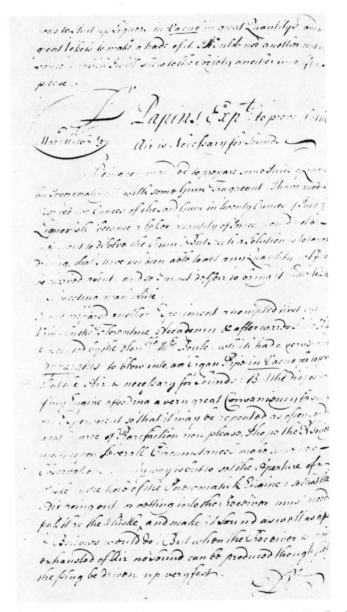

Plate 8. Description of an experiment on sound propagation by Denis Papin, 1685 (item VI-13, p. 166)

VI-14. Papin, [Denis].

Experiment of Producing Sounds by Factitious Air. RBC: 6.167, [read] March 18, 1684/5.

Printed: Bir. X-48

Describes an experiment devised to determine whether sound will pass through air that is pumped into a receiver after a vacuum has been created.

1686-7

VI-15. The Minutes of the Dublin Society. RBC: 8.123-5, November 15, 1686-January 24, [1687].

Original: CP III-13

Ref.: EL II-48, PT I-34, RB VI-16

See II-48 for description.

1688

VI-16. Moulin, Allen.

Anatomicall Observations in the Heads of Severall Fowle made at Severall times. RBC: 7.111-116, read February 1, 1687/8.

Printed: PT I-34

Ref.: EL II-48, CP III-13, RB VI-15, JB X-53

See I-34 for description.

1698

VI-17. Wallis, [John].

A Question in Musick lately proposed to Dr. Wallis concerning the Division of the Monochord or Section of the Musicall Canon with his Answer to it. RBC: 7.280-85 [March 5, 1697/8; read March 15].

Printed: PT I-39

See I-39 for description.

VI-18. Wallis, John.
A letter . . . to Mr. Andrew Fletcher concerning the Strange Effects reported of Musick in former times beyond what it is to be found in latter Ages. RBC: 7.296-301, Oxford, August 18, 1698 [read Aug. 31].
Printed: PT I-41
Original: EL II-51

See I-41 for description.

VI-19. Halley, [Edmund].
Concerning the Motion of Light. RBC: 7.391-4, [1698].

Includes comparison of sound and light -- the nature and speed of the waves.

VI-20. Walker, [Joshua].
Some Experiments & Observations concerning Sounds. RBC: 8.53-58, [1698].
Printed: PT I-43

See I-43 for description. (Some minor differences in text.)

ca. 1702-06

VI-21. [Anonymous.]
A Description of the Lapland Drums and the manner of using them; of the Negroes burying their Dead and their way of telling whether they come to untimely Death. RBC: 9.144-45 [ca. 1702-06].
Ref.: Bir. X-40

Describes drums used by natives in Norway near Yarpin. Form and ceremonial use of instrument discussed. A drum from Lapland had been donated to the Society by Mr. Heisig on Dec. 14, 1681 (see ref.), and it is listed in the Ms. catalogs of the Society's museum (catalog B, Ms. 414, "Artificial Curiosities," fol. 7, and catalog D, Ms. 416, section 16, p. 5).

1717

VI-22. Felice [= Felici], Giovanni Battista.
Extract of a Letter written in 1717 . . . concerning the Singing of the Cicada to Pascasio Gianetti M.D., Lecturer of Physick in ordinary at the University of Pisa. Taken from the Giornale de' Letterati d'Italia of 1724. RBC: 17.1-12, 1717 (read March 3, 1731/2).

Article summarizes Felici's work on the cicada. Discards former theories about what causes the song of the insect and shows that the vibration of thin membranes in the belly cavity causes the sound. Discusses figures which are not present.

1722

VI-23. Halley, [Edmund].
Of a Valve near the Drum of the Ear. RBC: 11.186-7, [read] February 22, 1721[/2].
Original: CP III-28
Ref.: PT I-65 and JB X-75
Ed.: Hal., pp. 168-69.

See III-28 for description.

1727

VI-24. Hooke, Robert.
A curious Dissertation concerning the Causes of the Power & Effects of Musick . . . . Communicated by W[illiam] Derham. RBC: 13.3-13, [ca. 1676] (read December 14, 1727).
Original: CP III-29
Ed: Gouk, see III-29
Ref.: JB X-76

See III-29 for description.

1728

VI-25. (Book review): [Jean-Philippe] Rameau, *Nouveau système de musique théorique* (Paris, 1726). A Summary Account of a new System of Music by M. Rameau formerly Organist of the Cathedral Church of Clermont in Auvergne. RBC: 13.19-24, read January 18, 1727[/8].
Original: CP III-30
Ed.: Miller; see CP III-30

Review by Brook Taylor. See III-30 for description.

VI-26. Carrillo, Jos[eph] Israel.
An Account of an uncommon Phenomenon of the Verbascum in flower, being part of a Letter . . . to Isaac de Segueyra Samuda. RBC: 14.419-22, Tunis, August 25, 1728 (read April 30, 1730), Latin.
Original and trans.: EL II-63
Ref.: JB X-77

See II-63 for description.

1732

VI-27. (Book review): [John Christopher Pepusch and] James Lord Paisley, *A Treatise on harmony, containing the chief Rules for Composing in two, three and four Parts: dedicated to all Lovers of Musick by an Admirer of this agreeable Science* (the Right Honourable James Lord Paisley F.R.S.), [2nd ed.], London, 1731. An account of a Book. RBC: 16.350-57, read February 17, 1731/2.

> Original: CP III-31
> Ref.: JB X-78

> This source identifies Paisley as author of the treatise. See III-31 for description.

1739

VI-28. Cleland, Archibald.

> A Description of Needles made for the Eyes . . . ; [and] the following Instruments . . . proposed to remedy some kind of Deafness proceeding from Obstructions in the external and internal auditory Passages. RBC: 21.246-52, read Feb. 1, 1738[/9].

> > Printed: PT I-66
> > Ref.: JB X-80

> See I-66 for description.

VI-29. Beighton, Henry.

> > Of Sound. RBC: 21.316-19, read May 10, 1739.
> > Ref.: EL II-65, LB V-33

> Relates experiments designed to demonstrate that sounds of different frequencies and volumes travel at the same speed. Movement of sound in air compared to movement of pendulum. Paper dated June 1725 (see *Register Book* prefatory material).

VI-30. Beighton, Henry.

> Of the Force of Sound. RBC: 21.319-320, read May 10, 1739.
>
> Ref.: EL II-65, LB V-33

> Describes experiment in which a glass was broken by a tone from a flute.

VII. GENERAL MANUSCRIPTS

(Archive code GM)

This collection comprises manuscripts in the possession of the Royal Society, but not necessarily related to its proceedings. It includes sets of miscellaneous correspondence, Oldenburg's commonplace book, and other, similar materials. A catalog of the collection, by J. O. Halliwell, was published in 1840 and appears in the same volume as Shuckard's catalog of the *Early Letters*.

1659

VII-1. [Letter of] Henry Oldenburg to Saporta. GM: 1, fol. 47r/v, 48r, May 6, 1659 [Julian: April 26], French, 3pp.
Ed: Old. no. 118

Ms. copy of letter in Oldenburg's commonplace book. Part of letter describes a comparison made by Descartes between the functioning of animals' bodies and that of church organs.

VIII. BOYLE LETTERS AND PAPERS

(Archive codes BL -- Boyle Letters, and
BP -- Boyle Papers)

The archives of the Royal Society house large sets of letters and papers by, or belonging to, individual scientists. The Boyle Letters are bound in seven volumes and are generally arranged alphabetically by author. Only volume 7, which contains the most scientifically significant material, is an exception to this rule. This volume comprises 57 letters arranged chronologically by its compiler Henry Miles, who also added a table of contents with summaries of each item. The Boyle Letters were cataloged by R. E. W. Maddison, "A Tentative Index of the Correspondence of the Honourable Robert Boyle, F.R.S.," Royal Society *Notes and Records* 13 (1958): 128-201. For each item, that index cites date, correspondents, manuscript source, and any printed version. Some of the letters were published in Thomas Birch's edition of Boyle's works (1772).

The Boyle Papers are housed in 46 guardbooks, cataloged under four subject headings: philosophy, science, theology, and miscellaneous. Each volume is provided with a rough table of contents; volume 41 contains the treatise by John Birchensha.

Index listings below designate source (BL -- Boyle Letters, or BP -- Boyle Papers), volume, and item number. Titles in parentheses are taken from Miles' index.

1661

VIII-1. (A letter from Robert Southwell Esq. to Mr. Henry Oldenburg concerning some extraordinary Ecchoes.) BL: vol. 7, no. 56, Kinsaile, Sept. 19, 1661, 2pp.
>Printed: PT I-72
>Ref: JB X-86
>Ed.: Old. no. 238

>See I-72 for description.

1662

VIII-2. [Letter from] John Wallis to Robert Moray. BL: vol. 5, no. 170, Oxford, May 6, 1662, 1p.
>Ref.: PT I-5, JB X-2A
>Ed.: Boyle Works, vol. 6, p. 455

>Wallis offers to bring the deaf mute to whom he has been teaching speech to Moray for a demonstration. Wallis appears to have brought the man to the Royal Society on May 21, 1662 (see JB ref.).

1661-5

VIII-3. Matters and Experiment[s] recommended to the care of Mr. Robert Boyle. BL: vol. 7, no. 54, 1661-65, 2pp.

>Listing of experiments only. Nos. 5 and 23 (1662 and 1665) pertain to velocity of sound and "expts of sound and musick" performed in Oxford.

1669

VIII-4. [Letter from] John Wallis to Robert Boyle. BL: vol. 5, no. 174, Oxford, July 17, 1669, 4pp.
Ed.: Boyle Works, vol. 6, p. 458

Refers to the dedication of a theater in Oxford; includes reference to music played.

[before 1670]

VIII-5. A Coppy [*sic*] of a Letter [from Robert Boyle?] to Mr. Hartlib of Accoustiques and Olfactiques, etc. BL: vol. 7, no. 55, [before 1670], 7pp.

Discusses mechanical aids to hearing, music of the spheres, and adverse effects of loud noise on hearing. Describes a procedure for developing acoustic devices and presents a series of suggestions for studying problems of hearing and smelling.

1670

VIII-6. A letter of Monsr. Morhofius . . . to H. Oldenburg concerning a way of breaking of glasses with a certain sound. BL: vol. 7, no. 27, Nov. 3, 1670, 4pp., Latin.
Ed.: Old. no. 1542
Ref.: JB X-25

Daniel George Morhof relates experiment in which glass was broken by a high-pitched voice.

[before 1672]

VIII-7. Birchensha, John.

A Compendious Discourse of the Principles of the Practicall & Mathematicall Partes of Musick. Also, Directions how to make any kind of Tune, or Ayre, without the helpe of the Voice, or any other Musicall Instrument. Written . . . for the use of the Honorable Robert Boyle, Esq. BP: XLI, no. 1 [after 1664, before 1672], 38pp.

Ref.: LB V-3, PT I-16, CP III-12

Contains 13 chapters on the practical aspects of music (keys, intervals, consonance and dissonance, etc.), 21 chapters on the mathematical aspects of music, and a final section presenting instructions on composition in one part only. Includes musical examples. Presumably an early version of the "Syntagma musicae" discussed in I-16 and III-12. (See Plate 9.)

1676

VIII-8. [Letter from] S. Pache to Boyle. BL: vol. 4, no. 96, Caen, July 13 [Julian: July 3], 1676, 3pp., French.

Mentions the university and teachers of guitar and dance at Caen.

[before 1691]

VIII-9. [Letter from] Vincenzo Viviani. BL: vol. 5, no. 168, [before 1691], 3pp., Italian.

On measuring the speed of sound through experiments with artillery.

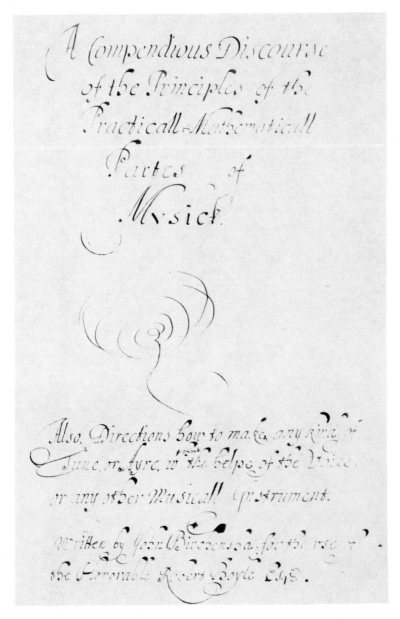

Plate 9. Title page of John Birchensha's *Compendious Discourse* (item VIII-7)

IX. EXTRA MANUSCRIPTS

This five-volume set contains various papers, many of substantial length, not bound into other collections. At the front of each volume is a hand-written list of its contents. A small number of important papers relative to the present study are found in these volumes.

[ca. 1660]

IX-1. Boyle, Robert.

Mr. Boyl's [*sic*] experiments. Extra manuscripts: vol. 3, no. 2, [ca. 1660], 12pp.

Item 26 proposes experiments on sound, including (1) testing sympathetic vibrations between a string placed in a receiver and another one outside the receiver, and (2) pumping air into a receiver that contains a bellows. These proposals also made in his *New Experiments Physico-Mechanical* (pub. 1660; see Birch, *The Works of Robert Boyle,* vol. 1, p. 64).

1665

IX-2. [Anonymous.]

Tractatus Musicus. Extra manuscripts: vol. 4, no. 1 (dated Rome, Aug. 6, 1665), 32 pp., Latin.

An incomplete treatise on acoustics that deals with the nature of sound, vibrating bodies, the organ of hearing, harmonic ratios, and the derivation of musical intervals. (See Plate 10.)

1669

IX-3. Holder, William.

Elements of Speach. An Essay of Enquirie into the Naturall Production of Letters. Extra manuscripts: vol. 2, no. 6 (read Feb. 25, 1668[/9]), 37pp.

Ref.: JB X-21

Includes discussion of the human organs of hearing and of voice production. Closes wth an "Appendix Concerning Persons Deafe

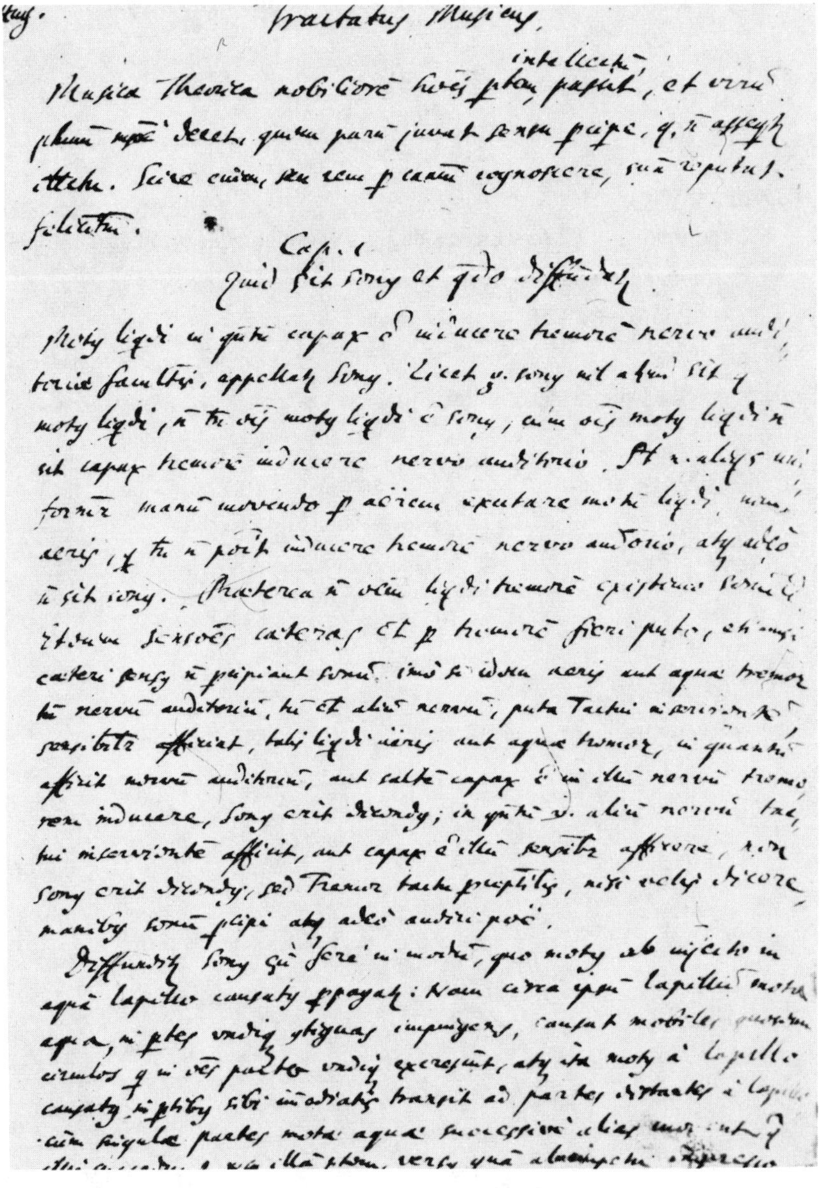

Plate 10. Beginning of the anonymous *Tractatus Musicus*, 1665 (item IX-2, p. 1)

& Dumb." Published by J. Martyn, "printer to the Royal Society," 1669.

1708

IX-4. Derham, W[illiam].

Experimenta et Observationes de Soni Motu aliisque ad id attinentibus.

Extra manuscripts: vol. 5, no. 3 (read Feb. 18, 1707[/8]), 60pp.

Printed: PT I-58

See I-58 for description.

X. JOURNAL BOOK

(Minutes of the Society's meetings; archive codes JBO -- Journal Book Original or JBC -- Journal Book Copy)

The minutes of the Society's meetings are preserved in a *Journal Book,* which, like the *Letter* and *Register Books,* exists in both an original and a manuscript copy. Thomas Birch published the minutes in full for the years 1660 to 1686 in his *History of the Royal Society of London* (London, 1756-57). His transcript is very faithful to the *Journal Book;* it differs from the original minutes only in clarification of details and by the occasional inclusion of complete papers.

In the early years, the minutes are very sketchy, often merely listing the titles of papers read; later entries are generally more extensive. Also noteworthy of the early minutes are the frequent descriptions of experiments performed at the meetings, without citation of participants. Later references are more likely to summarize papers read than to detail actual demonstrations performed before the members.

The Society possesses a manuscript index of the *Journal Book* compiled by Martin Folkes, who served as the organization's president from 1741 to 1752. Folkes lists the date of each session, the papers read, the archival sources in which pertinent documents were placed *(Letter Book, Register Book,* etc.), and if published, the issues of the *Transactions* in which given items appear. The index runs to 1738, but proves not to be totally reliable.

The present listing, while comprehensive, makes no attempt to include every reference to music or acoustics in the minutes, however remote or abbreviated. *Journal Book* entries of substantial length are always noted; single-sentence entries, however, are limited to those items which are not referenced elsewhere in the present catalog, or those which provide information other than merely the date read. In the case of papers referenced elsewhere in this book, the dates read (derived solely from the *Journal Book)* are listed together with the papers cited, rather than in this section.

Papers presented over the course of several meetings are cited only once, normally on the date the reading was completed; it was customary to enter a summary of the entire paper into the minutes at that point. Related entries are combined into a single listing in the following cases: X-12, X-20, X-25, X-34, X-37, X-59, X-60, X-64A, and X-65. *Journal Book* references up to 1686 are derived from Birch; thereafter, citations are to the JBC by volume and page numbers.

1661

X-1. Brouncker, William, and Robert Boyle. Bir: vol. 1, pp. 8-9, Jan. 2, 1660/1.
Ms. copy: RB VI-1

Questions proposed, to be sent to Teneriffe; includes one on sound.

1662

X-1A. Wilkins, John. Bir: vol. 1, p. 68, Jan. 1, 1661/2.

Wilkins brings in his "engine for hearing." May be the ivory otacousticon listed in Grew's *Musaeum Regalis Societatis* . . . and Royal Society Mss. 413 and 417 (see Introduction, section 2).

X-2. Rooke, Lawrence, and John Birchensha. Bir: vol. 1, pp. 80-81, April 16 and 23, 1662.

April 16: Rooke reads a paper on music brought in by John Brooke. April 23: a committee is formed to examine "the synopsis" of Birchensha, presumably the paper read on April 16.

X-2A. Wallis, John. Bir: vol. 1, pp. 83-84, May 14 and 21, 1662.
Ref.: PT I-5, BL VIII-2

May 14: Wallis reads account of teaching speech to a deaf-mute. May 21: Wallis brings the man to the Royal Society for a demonstration.

X-3. Powle, Henry. Bir: vol. 1, pp. 120-23 + plate, Nov. 5, 1662.
Original document: CP III-6
Ms. copy: RB VI-3
Ref.: JB X-5

Powle's paper on the whispering place at Gloucester is read. Entire paper printed in Birch.

X-4. Birchensha, John, and William Brouncker. Bir: vol. 1, pp. 125-26, Nov. 12 and 19, 1662.

Nov. 12: Charleton presents a paper on music by Birchensha. Nov. 19: Brouncker criticizes Birchensha's paper.

X-5. Moray, Robert, and William Wynde. Bir: vol. 1, p. 132, Nov. 26, 1662.
Original documents: CP III-7 and III-9
Ref.: JB X-3

Moray submits paper on echoes; Wynde presents draft of whispering place in Gloucester, as described by Powle in ref.

X-6. Moray, Robert. Bir: vol. 1, pp. 137-38 + plate, Dec. 3, 1662.
Original document: CP III-9
Ms. copy: RB VI-5

Moray's account of an echo in Scotland read. Entire paper printed in Birch.

1663

X-7. Wallis, John. Bir: vol. 1, p. 205, Feb. 25, 1662/3.

Relates case of a man cured of deafness by a loud noise.

X-8. Brouncker, William, Robert Moray, Alexander Bruce, [and Robert Hooke]. Bir: vol. 1, pp. 208-12, March 18, 1662/3.
Ms. copy of original: RB VI-6

Account of experiments on the Thames read. Entire paper printed in Birch; experiments on sound, pp. 211-12.

1664

X-9. Moray, Robert. Bir: vol. 1, p. 369, Jan. 6, 1663/4.

Relates observation from Duke of York [James Stuart, 2nd son of Charles I] that the sound of a gunshot is muted when the wind is from the east.

X-10. Moray, Robert, et al. Bir: vol. 1, p. 416, April 20, 1664.
Ref.: JB X-11

Discussion of a man [i.e., Birchensha] who discovered errors in musical scales and proportions. Committee appointed to investigate the claims.

X-11. Birchensha, John. Bir: vol. 1, p. 418, April 27, 1664.
Original document: LB V-3
Ref.: JB X-10

Birchensha's paper on his proposed treatise read and discussed. Favorable response; committee instructed to continue its review.

X-12. [No specific author]. Bir: vol. 1, pp. 446-47, 449, 451, 453, and 455-57; July 6, 13, 20, and 27, and August 3, 1664.

Acoustical experiments on the velocity of sound and on the vibration of strings described; some conducted on the monochord. Evelyn mentions concert by Birchensha on August 3, presumably after the meeting (Evelyn, *Diary*, vol. 3, p. 377).

X-13. Birchensha, John. Bir: vol. 1, p. 458, Aug. 10, 1664.

Birchensha participates in an experiment using the monochord, which is designed to compare mathematical tuning with tuning by ear. Pepys mentions concert by Birchensha on this day, presumably after the meeting (Pepys, *Diary*, vol. 5, p. 238).

X-14. Huygens, Christiaan, Robert Moray, and John Birchensha. Bir: vol. 1, p. 460, Aug. 17, 1664.

> Original document (Huygens): EL II-6
> Ms. copy: LB V-4
> Ed.: Huy. no. 1250

Huygens' letter to Moray, which includes a reference to the monochord, is read, and Moray proposes an experiment to study vibrations of "hard bodies sounding." Proposal made for Birchensha to test pitch variation in gut strings.

X-15. Goddard, Jonathan. Bir: vol. 1, p. 468, Sept. 14, 1664.

> Ref.: X-14

Goddard suggests improvements on Moray's experiment proposed in X-14.

X-16. Moray, Robert. Bir: vol. 1, pp. 475-76, Oct. 12, 1664.

> Ref.: EL II-8

Moray's experiment on "hard bodies sounding" was tried and found useless. Birch adds a footnote about a performance on an Archiviole at this meeting, which is described by Oldenburg (see ref.).

1666

X-17. Boyle, Robert. Bir: vol. 2, p. 83, April 18, 1666.

Boyle asked to give account of acoustical experiments performed in Oxford the previous summer.

1668

X-18. Pope, Walter, and Robert Hooke. Bir: vol. 2, pp. 257-58, March 19, 1668.
Ms. copy of original document (Hooke): RB VI-7

Pope and Hooke report on book of Florentine experiments, including those on sound; Christopher Merret and William Balle are asked to report on it also. Boyle is asked to repeat Florentine experiment on sound, and Lawrence Rooke's measurement of the speed of sound at 1 mile in 4 seconds is mentioned. Hooke describes a device for collecting the wind and is asked to prepare an otacousticon. Hooke's entire paper printed in Birch.

X-19. Brouncker, William. Bir: vol. 2, p. 261, March 26, 1668.

Proposes experiment to determine velocity of sound.

X-20. Hooke, Robert. Bir: vol. 2, pp. 261-63 and 271; April 2, 9, and 16, 1668.

Hooke demonstrates a glass otacousticon and tin and glass "receivers" for magnifying sounds. Pepys, commenting on the April 2 meeting, describes the glass receiver as merely a broken bottle, although he claims it was effective (Pepys, *Diary*, vol. 9, p. 146).

1669

X-21. Holder, William. Bir: vol. 2, pp. 350 and 352, February 25, 1668/9.
Ref.: Extra Mss., IX-3

Holder presents discourse on his *Elements of Speech*. Society agrees to print it.

X-22. [No specific author]. Bir: vol. 2, p. 355, March 11, 1669.

Various Fellows present observations on dances and musical airs associated with curing tarantula bites.

X-23. Desgabetz, Robert. Bir: vol. 2, pp. 409-10, Dec. 2, 1669.
Original document: EL II-16
Ms. copy: LB V-5

Moray presents paper from Desgabetz with several inventions (including a new musical instrument) but questions the value of them.

1670

X-24. Moray, Robert, and Samuel Morland. Bir: vol. 2, pp. 440-41, June 9, 1670.

Moray mentions the invention of a speaking trumpet by Morland.

X-25. Morhof, Daniel George, and Robert Hooke. Bir: vol. 2, pp. 450 and 453, Nov. 3 and 17, 1670.
Original document (Morhof): BL VIII-6
Ed.: Old. no. 1542

Nov. 3: Morhof's experiment of breaking a glass with a sonorous voice is described to Society. Nov. 17: Hooke reports that he tried Morhof's experiment and that the glass sounded but did not break. Morhof's work later published as *Epistola de scypho vitreo per certum humanae vocis sonum rupto . . . dissertatio* (Kiel, 1672).

1671

X-26. Pardies, Ignace-Gaston, Robert Boyle, Robert Moray, and Robert Hooke. Bir: vol. 2, pp. 500-01, Dec. 14 and 21, 1671.
Ms. copy of original document (Pardies): LB V-6

Letter of Pardies read, in which he questions conclusions of Florentine experiments on sound. Subsequent discussion includes Boyle's comments on experiments with sound in a vacuum and Moray's relation of one who could "make two notes by tuning only one string." Hooke describes a new tablature. (Evelyn mentions Hooke reading his "new method on the Art of Musique"; Evelyn *Diary,* vol. 3, p. 599.)

1672

X-27. Cornelio, Thomas. Bir: vol. 3, pp. 9-10, Feb. 8 and 15, 1671/2.
Original document: EL II-25

Cornelio's letter on tarantula bites read and discussed.

X-28. Hooke, Robert. Bir: vol. 3, pp. 10-15, Feb. 15, 1671/2.
Ms. copy of original (Hooke): RB VI-9

Hooke presents paper refuting Newton's theories on light; includes comparison with sound (p. 11). Hooke's paper printed in Birch.

X-29. Conyers, John. Bir: vol. 3, p. 51, June 5, 1672.
Ref.: PT I-27, JB X-30

Conyers presents a speaking trumpet to the members.

X-30. Goddard, Jonathan, John Conyers, Robert Hooke, and Isaac Vossius. Bir:

vol. 3, pp. 54-55, June 19, 1672.
Ref.: PT I-27, JB X-29

Figures of speaking trumpets shown by Hooke, Conyers, Goddard. Vossius describes method of giving bells a sweeter sound.

X-31. Hooke, Robert, and John Conyers. Bir: vol. 3, p. 55, June 26, 1672.

Describes testing of Hooke's and Conyers' speaking trumpets. Hooke's found to be the better.

1674

X-32. Petty, William. Bir: vol. 3, pp. 156-57, Nov. 26, 1674.
Ms. copy of original document: RB VI-10

Petty presents discourse on duplicate and subduplicate proportion. Summary printed in Birch.

1675

X-33. Hooke, Robert. Bir: vol. 3, pp. 193-94, March 11, 1674/5.

Comparison of sound and light.

X-34. Newton, Isaac. Bir: vol. 3, pp. 247-60, Dec. 9, 1675.
Ms. Copy of original: RB VI-11
Ed.: New., nos. 145 and 146

Newton's discourse on light read; includes comparisons with sound (pp. 248, 251, and 258). Entire paper printed in Birch. Later minor reference to the division of a musical string in a paper by Newton presented on Dec. 16 (Bir., vol. 3, p. 262).

1676

X-35. Birchensha, John. Bir: vol. 3, pp. 295-96, Feb. 10, 1675/6.
    Ref.: CP III-12

Birchensha shows his scale, table of intervals, and system of keys. Summary printed in Birch. Society urges him to publish his system.

1677

X-36. Wallis, John. Bir: vol. 3, p. 337, March 22, 1676/7.
    Original document: EL II-44
    Printed: PT I-26

Wallis' letter to Oldenburg on nodes and sympathetic vibrations read. Summary in the minutes.

1680

X-37. Hooke, Robert, and Christopher Wren. Bir: vol. 4, p. 46, July 8, 1680.

An experiment performed at the meeting showed that a glass struck with a viol bow produced tones sounding in octaves, fifths, etc. A similar experiment was performed on March 14, 1683 (see Bir, vol. 4, p. 194).

X-38. [No specific author]. Bir: vol. 4, p. 48, July 22, 1680.

Experiments are described on the sounds produced in a glass struck with a bow.

1681

X-39. Hooke, Robert. Bir: vol. 4, p. 96, July, 27, 1681.

Hooke shows how to make a musical sound using the teeth of brass wheels.

X-40. Heisig. Bir: vol. 4, pp. 111-13, Dec. 7 and 14, 1681.
Ref.: RB VI-21

Heisig, a "Swedish gentleman," presents a Lapland drum to the Society. (Item subsequently listed in manuscript catalogs of museum; see ref.)

1683

X-41. Plot, Robert. Bir: vol. 4, pp. 183-84, Feb. 14, 1682/3.
Ms. copy of original document: LB V-8

Letter by Plot read, in which is described a cure for deafness by exposure to loud bells. Entire letter printed in Birch.

X-42. Mariotte, Edme. Bir: vol. 4, p. 205, May 16, 1683.
Ms. copy of original document: LB V-9

Francis Aston reads letter from Mariotte, part of which deals with the anatomy of the ear.

1684

X-43. Huntington, Robert. Bir: vol. 4, pp. 246-49, Jan. 16, 1683/4.
Original document: EL II-46
Ms. copy: LB V-11

Huntington's letter, describing meetings in Dublin, read. Includes references to Narcissus Marsh's paper on sound and Allen Moulin's account of the anatomy of the ear. Entire letter printed in Birch.

X-44. Marsh, Narcissus. Bir: vol. 4, p. 261, Feb. 27, 1683/4.
 Ms. copy of original document: LB V-12
 Printed: PT I-30

 Marsh's paper on sound read. Summary in minutes.

X-45. Molyneux, William; John Hoskins. Bir: vol. 4, pp. 272-73 and 275, March 26, 1684.
 Ms. copy of original document (Molyneux): LB V-13

 Letter from Molyneux read, containing minutes of the Dublin Society, Feb. 10-March 10, 1683/4. Minutes printed in full in Birch, including information on presentation by Allen Moulin on anatomy of the ear. Hoskins comments on the sound of the string of a cross-bow.

X-45A. Petty, William. Bir: vol. 4, p. 323, July 23, 1684.

 Minutes of Dublin Society from June 9 to July 24, 1684, read. On July 7, Petty suggested testing the effectiveness of Morland's speaking trumpet by putting a watch in it.

X-46. Papin, Denis. Bir: vol. 4, pp. 335-37, Nov. 26, 1684.
 Ms. copy of original document: RB VI-12

 Papin comments on Florentine experiments, including one on sound. Paper printed in Birch.

1685

X-47. Papin, Denis. Bir: vol. 4, p. 379, March 11, 1684/5.
Ms. copy of original document: RB VI-13

Experiment with organ pipe described. Entire paper printed in Birch.

X-48. Papin, Denis. Bir: vol. 4, pp. 381-82, March 18, 1684/5.
Ms. copy of original document: RB VI-14

Experiment on sound in a vacuum described. Entire paper printed in Birch.

X-49. Musgrave, William, and William Petty. Bir: vol. 4, pp. 397-98, May 6, 1685.
Ms. copy of original document: LB V-16

Musgrave's letter, to which is appended a list of scientific instruments compiled by Petty, is read. Petty's list, which includes musical or acoustic devices, is printed in full.

1686

X-50. Justel, Henri. Bir: vol. 4, p. 493, July 7, 1686.

Letter from Justel describes some African instruments. Summary in minutes.

1687

X-51. Dublin Society; Edward Tyson et al. Bir: vol. 4, p. 546, July 13, 1687.
Ref.: EL II-48

Minutes of Dublin Society read; reference to the organ of hearing in birds. Further discussion by Tyson and others recorded in minutes.

1688

X-52. Hoskins, John, and Christopher Wren. JBC: vol. 7, p. 77, Jan. 18, 1687/8.

Hoskins states Wren's opinion that a function of pillars in churches is to help the hearing by preventing echoes.

X-53. Moulin, Allen. JBC: vol. 7, pp. 82-83, Feb. 1, 1687/8.
Document printed: PT I-34
Ms. copy: RB VI-16

Moulin reads anatomical paper on the heads of birds, largely concerned with eyes and ears. Summarized in minutes.

1689

X-54. Hooke, Robert. JBC: vol. 7, p. 216, July 10, 1689.

Hooke discusses calculation of speed of sound from tests using gunshots.

X-55. Hill, Abraham. JBC: vol. 7, p. 219, July 17, 1689.

Hill hypothesizes that the speed of sound increases "upon continuance of the same sound."

1691

X-56. Halley, Edmund, and Robert Southwell. JBC: vol. 9, pp. 56-57, Sept. 30, 1691.

Original document: CP III-14

Halley reads paper on transmission of sound through water. Ensuing discussion by Southwell recorded in minutes.

1697

X-57. Southwell, Robert, and Vincenzo Viviani. JBC: vol. 9, p. 60, July 13, 1697.

Southwell discusses communication from Viviani regarding Galileo's work in measuring time with a pendulum and its use for keeping time in music.

1699

X-58. Sloane, Hans. JBC: vol. 9, p. 134, March 8, 1698/9.

Sloane comments on a dog that could hear with a punctured tympanum. Discussion by William Cowper.

X-59. Hooke, Robert; Edward Tyson and Raymond Vieussens. JBC: vol. 9, p. 136, March 15, 1698/9.
Ref.: PT I-46, EL II-54 and LB V-23

Hooke comments that the function of the tympanic membrane is to serve as "a Skreen to the Nerve of hearing." Tyson asked to review Raymond Vieussens' paper on ear; discussion recorded in minutes. Later minor reference (Dec. 4, 1700): Hans Sloane reads a letter from Vieussens to Dr. Sylvester containing some remarks on the ear (JBC 9, p. 235).

X-60. Hooke, Robert, and Jean de Hautefeuille. JBC: vol. 9, p. 154, May 31, 1699.

Original document: CP III-16

Hooke reads his account of Hautefeuille's book, including information on sound transmission through solid bodies. Discussion by Southwell, et al. Later minor reference (Dec. 2, 1702): an extract of de Hautefeuille's writings is read; part of this concerns the speaking trumpet (JBC 10, p. 8).

1701

X-61. Wanley, Humfrey, and John Wallis. JBC: vol. 9, p. 254, April 16, 1701.

Wanley shows ancient Greek manuscript containing collection of hymns and anthems. Two reviews of manuscripts read, one by Wanley and one by Wallis.

1703

X-62. Shadwell, John, et al. JBC: vol. 10, p. 51, Nov. 17, 1703.

Shadwell relates case of deafness cured by drinking bath waters; discussion by Bemboe and John Woodward entered in minutes. (See Plate 11.)

1704

X-63. Hauksbee, Francis. JBC: vol. 10, p. 66, March 8, 1703/4.
    Ref.: PT I-51, CP III-19

Hauksbee shows three experiments, one of which deals with a bell in a vacuum.

X-64. Hauksbee, Francis. JBC: vol. 10, p. 68, March 15, 1703/4.
    Ref.: PT I-52, CP III-20

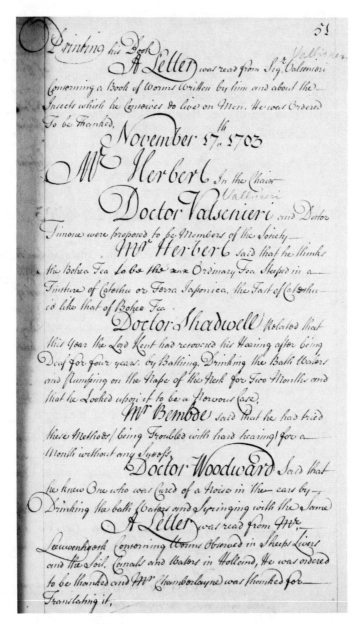

Plate 11. Minutes for the meeting of November 17, 1703 (see item X-62, p. 51)

Hauksbee demonstrates his air pump and shows an experiment with bell in a near vacuum.

1705

X-64A. Derham, William. JBC: vol. 10, pp. 97 and 102, Feb. 21 and April 18, 1705.

> Ref.: PT I-58

Letters from Derham on experiments with sound are read. Later related references include: Nov. 20, 1706 -- another paper by Derham on sound propagation is read (JBC vol. 10, p. 142); Feb. 25, 1707/8 -- Halley commends the accuracy of Derham's paper (see I-58; JBC vol. 10, p. 177).

X-65. Salmon, Thomas. JBC: vol. 10, pp. 110-11, June 27 and July 3, 1705.

> Ref.: PT I-56
> Original: CP III-22

June 27: Salmon shows a viol fingerboard with new placement of the frets to produce more mathematically accurate tuning. July 3: experiment of same with a performance of a lesson for two viols and a Corelli sonata using two violins and two viols. Performers: Frederick and Christian Steffkin and Gasparo Visconti. Later minor reference (Oct. 31): "Some letters and papers from Mr. Salmon Concerning Musick were read" (JBC 10, pp. 112-13).

1709

X-66. Hauksbee, Francis, and Patrick [?] Blair. JBC: vol. 10, pp. 219-20, June 29 and July 6, 1709.

June 29: Hauksbee demonstrates experiment with sound of brass wire. July 6: Blair sends description and figure of organ of hearing in elephants.

1710

X-67. Geekie, Alexander. JBC: vol. 10, p. 246, Nov. 15, 1710.

Geekie shows aural device made in France to aid hearing.

X-68. Hunt, Henry [?]. JBC: vol. 10, p. 247, Nov. 22, 1710.

Hunt brings in diagram of acoustic device presented by Geekie at previous meeting.

1712

X-69. Long, Roger [?]. JBC: vol. 10, pp. 408-09, June 19, 1712.

Long shows a new musical instrument -- a combined harp and spinet. Description of the instrument entered in the minutes. Harp and spinet can be played alone or combined; dynamic variation is possible.

1713

X-70. Lhuyd, Edward, and Francis Nevill. JBC: vol. 10, pp. 446-48, Jan. 29, 1712/3.
Document printed: PT I-64

Letter from Lhuyd (Dec. 17, 1699), which includes description of ancient copper trumpets, is read. Communication from Nevill (Dec. 29, 1712) contains sketch of these trumpets. Discussion following presentation is also entered in minutes.

1715

X-71. Douglas, James, and Hans Sloane. JBC: vol. 11, p. 66, May 19, 1715.

Douglas' paper, in which he describes a canal leading from the ear to the palate, is read. Summary of paper and of subsequent discussion by Sloane included in the minutes.

X-72. Aston, Francis. JBC: vol. 11, p. 67, May 26, 1715.

Aston comments on deaf man who could feel sound vibrations with his mouth well enough to tune an instrument.

X-73. Desaguilliers, John Theophilus. JBC: vol. 11, p. 85, Nov. 3, 1715.

Desaguilliers demonstrates a method of making vibrations of a bell apparent to both the eye and the ear.

1718

X-74. Desaguilliers, John Theophilus. JBC: vol. 11, p. 249, June 12, 1718.

Desaguilliers discusses a hearing aid recently invented in France by Father Sebastian (= Jean Truchet).

1722

X-75. Halley, Edmund. JBC: vol. 12, pp. 207-08, Feb. 22, 1721[/2].
Original document: CP III-28
Ms copy: RB VI-23
Ed.: Hal., pp. 168-69

Includes summary of Halley's experiment by which he concludes that there must be a valve near the ear drum.

1727

X-76. Derham, William, and Robert Hooke. JBC: vol. 13, pp. 153-55, Dec. 14, 1727.
> Original document: CP III-29
> Ms. copy: RB VI-24
> Ed.: Gouk. See III-29

Derham's letter (Jan. 24, 1725/6) accompanying Hooke's paper on the "Causes of the Power and Effects of Musick" is read. Summary of Hooke's paper entered in JB.

1730

X-77. Carrillo, Joseph Israel. JBC: vol. 13, pp. 466-67, April 30, 1730.
> Original document: EL II-63
> Ms. copy: RB VI-26

Includes brief summary and evaluation of Carrillo's letter from Tunis on a plant that responds to music.

1732

X-78. Hadley, John, on Paisley/Pepusch treatise. JBC: vol. 14, p. 73, Feb. 17, 1731[/2].
> Original document: CP III-31
> Ms. copy: RB VI-27

Hadley reads a communication from a friend which contains an abridgment of the Paisley/Pepusch treatise of 1731 along with a recommendation of it.

1737

X-79. Rameau, Jean-Philippe. JBC: vol. 16, pp. 131-32, Nov. 3, 1737.
Ms. copy of original document: LB V-34
Trans.: EL II-69

Rameau's letter accompanying his treatise *Génération harmonique* is read. Brief summary entered in the minutes.

1739

X-80. Cleland, Archibald. JBC: vol. 16, pp. 360-62, Feb. 1, 1738[/9].
Document printed: PT I-66
Ms. copy: RB VI-28

Cleland's account of new medical instruments for operations on the eyes and ears is read. Detailed summary of the paper and subsequent discussion by the President [Sloane] entered in the minutes.

1742

X-81. Douglas, James. JBC: vol. 17, pp. 377-78, March 18, 1741[/2].

Douglas reads Croonian lecture for 1741, which includes study of the Eustacian tube.

X-82. Desaguilliers, John Theophilus, and Jacques de Vaucanson. JBC: vol. 17, pp. 401-02, May 6, 1742.

Desaguilliers gives Society copies of printed pamphlet concerning a mechanical flute player being shown in London at the time. Pamphlet is a translation from the French of Vaucanson's *mémoire* presented to the Paris Academy. See Albert Cohen and

Leta E. Miller, *Music in the Paris Academy of Sciences, 1666-1793*, Detroit Studies in Music Bibliography, 43 (Detroit: Information Coordinators, 1979), items II-32 and VI-4. Trans. by Desagulliers published as *An Account of the Mechanism of an Automaton* (London: T. Parker, 1742).

1743

X-83. Nesbitt, Robert. JBC: vol. 18, p. 35, Feb. 17, 1742[/3].
Ref.: LP IV-3, IV-4

Nesbitt "produced some curious preparations of the Bones of the Ear" to refute claims made by Baster about discovery of a "process of the malleus." Nesbitt convinces Society that discovery had been made nearly 100 years earlier.

1745

X-84. Hamilton, James, 8th Earl of Abercorn. JBC: vol. 18, p. 369, Feb. 21, 1744/5.

Earl of Abercorn presents the Society with several hearing aids invented by his father (James Lord Paisley). These are not described in the minutes.

X-85. Baker, Henry, and Giuseppe Lorenzo Bruni. JBC: vol. 18, pp. 413-14, May 9, 1745.
Original document: LP IV-6

Baker's letter relates evidence from Bruni in Italy supporting the theory that fish can hear. Recounts story of an eel who killed itself after becoming restless at the sound of the cello.

1746

X-86. Miles, Henry, and Robert Southwell. JBC: vol. 19, pp. 123-24, June 5, 1746.

Original document: BL VIII-1

Printed: PT I-72

Miles reads two letters he found among Robert Boyle's papers. One is Southwell's 1661 letter to Oldenburg on echoes and whispering places (see PT I-72). Fairly detailed summary of letter entered in minutes.

1747

X-87. Creed, Rev., John Freke, and William Freeman. JBC: vol. 19, pp. 225-28, March 12, 1746[/7].

Document printed: PT I-74

Freke's letter is read, in which is enclosed Creed's paper describing a device which can notate music as it is played on a keyboard (see PT I-74). Freeman comments on its usefulness and limitations. Extensive description of machine and of subsequent discussion entered in minutes.

1748

X-88. Arderon, William. JBC: vol. 19, pp. 443-44, Feb. 11, 1747[/8].

Document printed: PT I-77

Arderon's letter, in which he concludes that fish have no sense of hearing, is read. Letter summarized in the minutes.

X-89. Brocklesby, Richard, and Jacob Theodore Klein. JBC: vol. 19, pp. 463-66, March 10, 1747[/8].

Document printed: PT I-78

Brocklesby's account of Klein's discourse, in which he concludes that fish *do* hear, is read. Account summarized in the minutes.

1751

X-90. Watson, William, and Benjamin Franklin. JBC: vol. 20, pp. 517-20, June 6, 1751.
   Original document: LP IV-12
   Printed: PT I-83

Watson's review of Benjamin Franklin's *Experiments and Observations on Electricity* is read. Extensive summary entered in minutes. Reference to use of electricity in relieving deafness (p. 519).

1755

X-91. Anonymous. JBC: vol. 22, pp. 106-08, April 17, 1755.
   Original document and trans.: LP IV-16
   Printed: PT I-86

Letter from a "learned gentleman" in Naples read. The letter, which recounts finding a music treatise at Herculaneum, is summarized in minutes.

X-92. Wathen, Jonathan. JBC: vol. 22, pp. 147-48, May 29. 1755.
   Document printed: PT I-87

Wathen's paper on restoring hearing read. Summary entered in minutes.

1756

X-93. Paderni, Camillo. JBC: vol. 22, pp. 277-84, Feb. 19, 1756.
Original document and trans.: LP IV-17
Printed: PT I-88

Reading of letter from Paderni to Thomas Hollis completed. Letter summarized in minutes, including discussion of music treatise by Philodemus (p. 282) and Robert Watson's comments on it (pp. 282-84).

1758

X-94. Brydone, Patrick. JBC: vol. 23, pp. 149-51, May 11, 1758.

Extract of a letter (dated Jan. 9, 1758) from Brydone to Robert Whytt read; letter discusses use of electricity to cure diseases and disabilities, including deafness.

1760

X-95. Eyles-Stiles, Francis Haskins. JBC: vol. 23, pp. 870-83, May 15, 1760.
Original document: LP IV-21
Printed: PT I-92

Reading of Eyles-Stiles' paper on Greek modes completed. Extensive summary entered in minutes.

1768

X-96. Court de Gebelin, Antoine. JBC: vol. 26, pp. 503-04, April 28, 1768.
Original document: LP IV-23
Ref.: JB X-97

Part of a letter (April 10, 1768) from Gebelin is read, in which he compares various languages, using musical analogies for vowels, consonants, etc. Summary in minutes.

1769

X-97. Court de Gebelin, Antoine. JBC: vol. 26, pp. 591-92, Jan. 26, 1769.
Original document: LP IV-24
Ref.: JB X-96

Minutes contain summary of letter from Gebelin (dated Oct. 7, 1768), in which he compares languages, using analogy of the musical scale.

1770

X-98. Barrington, Daines. JBC: vol. 26, pp. 731-34, Feb. 15, 1770.
Original document: LP IV-25
Printed: PT I-95

Barrington's paper on Mozart (dated Nov. 28, 1769) read; extensive summary, including some direct quotes from the article, entered in the minutes.

1773

X-99. Barrington, Daines. JBC: vol. 27, pp. 450-58, May 13, 1773.
Printed: PT I-99

Reading of Barrington's paper on bird songs completed. Extensive summary entered in minutes, including discussion of types of songs, how birds learn to sing, the vocal organ in birds, and Zeidler's composition for two bullfinches, written at the request of Barrington (but not included in minutes).

1775

X-100. Steele, Joshua. JBC: vol. 28, p. 151, Jan. 12, 1775.
Original document: LP IV-27
Printed: PT I-101

Steele's account of the pipes from the South Seas (given to the Society by Furneaux) is read. No summary of Steele's paper entered in minutes.

X-101. Steele, Joshua. JBC: vol. 28, p. 193, Feb. 23, 1775.
Original document: LP IV-27
Printed: PT I-102

Steele's account of the larger set of reed pipes and of the nose flute is read. Brief summary in minutes.

1779

X-102. Burney, Charles. JBC: vol. 29, pp. 350-54, Feb. 18, 1779.
Printed: PT I-106
Original document: LP IV-28

Burney's account of William Crotch, communicated to the Society by William Hunter, is read. Extensive summary entered in minutes.

1782

X-103. Guthrie, Mathew. JBC: vol. 30, pp. 589-95, June 6, 1782.
Original document: LP IV-30

Guthrie's paper on education in Russia read. Summary in minutes, with brief reference to music (p. 593).

X-104. Hunter, John. JBC: vol. 31, pp. 2-6, Nov. 14, 1782.
Original document: LP IV-31
Printed: PT I-108

Hunter's paper on hearing in fish read. Extensive summary in minutes.

1788

X-105. Cavallo, Tiberius. JBC: vol. 33, pp. 163-69, April 3, 1788.
Original document: LP IV-34
Printed: PT I-113

Reading of Cavallo's paper on temperament completed. Lengthy summary entered in minutes.

1796

X-106. Pearson, George. JBC: vol. 35, pp. 568-70, June 9, 1796.
Original document: LP IV-35
Printed: PT I-116

Reading of Pearson's paper on ancient instruments and tools completed. Summary entered in minutes.

1799

X-107. Home, Everard. JBC: vol. 36, pp. 508-16, Nov. 14, 1799.
Original document: LP IV-36
Printed: PT I-120

Reading of Home's Croonian lecture on the tympanic membrane concluded. Extensive summary in minutes.

1800

X-108. Young, Thomas. JBC: vol. 36, pp. 555-62, Feb. 6, 1800.
Original document: LP IV-37
Printed: PT I-121

Reading of Young's paper on sound and light concluded.
Extensive summary in minutes.

X-109. Cooper, Astley, and Everard Home. JBC: vol. 36, pp. 564-67, Feb. 13,
1800.
Original documents: LP IV-38 and IV-39
Printed: PT I-122 and I-123

Cooper's paper on destruction of tympanic membrane and
Home's comments on the paper are summarized in the minutes.

X-110. Volta, Alessandro. JBC: vol. 37, [8pp.], June 26, 1800.
Original document: LP IV-40
Printed: PT I-124

Paper on electricity by Professor Volta of Pavia read. Describes
device for exciting electrical shocks. Brief discussion of effects
of this on various senses, including hearing.

1801

X-111. Cooper, Astley. JBC: vol. 37, [3pp.], June 25, 1801.
Original document: LP IV-41
Printed: PT I-126

Cooper's paper on effects of destruction of tympanic membrane
communicated by Home. Summary in minutes.

X-112. Young, Thomas. JBC: vol. 37, [9pp.], Nov. 19, 1801.
　　　　Original document: LP IV-42
　　　　Printed: PT I-127

Reading of Young's Bakerian lecture on light and colors concluded. Includes comparison of sound and light. Summary in minutes.

X-113. Cooper, Astley. JBC: vol. 37, [8pp.], Nov. 30, 1801.
　　　　Ref.: I-126, X-111

Copley medal is awarded to Cooper for his work on curing deafness by perforating the ear drum. His 1801 paper is summarized. Minutes also describe a previous hypothesis of this technique made 80 years earlier by a Mr. Cheseldon.

1805

X-114. Carlisle, Anthony. JBC: vol. 38, pp. 491-98, April 4, 1805.
　　　　Original document: LP IV-43
　　　　Printed: PT I-128

Carlisle's paper on the stapes read. Detailed summary in minutes.

APPENDIX: AUTHORS, BRIEFLY IDENTIFIED

*(Principal sources for biographical information are given
in brackets immediately following the entry.)*

Abercorn, Earl of, see Hamilton.

Adams, Archibald (fl. 1706-09). Resident of Norwich.

Ames, Joseph (1689-1759), FRS 1743. English bibliographer and antiquary. Published work on the history of printing in England. [Brit.]

Arderon, William (1703-67), FRS 1745. Naturalist and clerk. Contributed to work on the microscope. [DNB]

Ashe, St. George (ca. 1658-1718), FRS 1685/6. Bishop in Ireland (Cloyne, Clogher and Derry). [H, DIB]

Aston, Francis (ca. 1645-ca. 1715), FRS 1678. Fellow of Trinity College, Cambridge, 1667ff. Secretary of R.S., 1681-85. [Bull, Old]

Aubrey, John (1626-97), FRS 1663. English diarist. Wrote "pen portraits" of contemporaries. Manuscript works on the natural history of Wiltshire and Oxfordshire, on education, Stonehenge, "Monumenta Britannica," etc. [Brit, HunA]

Baker, Henry (1698-1774), FRS 1740/1. Naturalist and poet; engaged extensively in education of deaf-mutes. Copley medal in 1744 for microscopic experiments. Established Bakerian lecture through bequeath to Royal Society. [DNB]

Balle, William (1627-90), FRS 1660. Astronomer. One of founders and first treasurer of Royal Society. [DNB]

Barrington, Daines (1727-1800), FRS 1767. Lawyer, antiquary, naturalist. Held various legal positions, including King's counsel. [DNB]

Baster, Job (1711-75), FRS 1738. Dutch physician. Published large number of works on botany and natural history. [NBU]

Beale, John (1603-ca. 1683), FRS 1663. Scientific writer; rector of Yeovil, chaplain to Charles II. [DNB]

Beck, Cave (1623-1706?). Writer on pasigraphy; grammar teacher. Author of *The Universal Character . . .* (1657). [DNB]

Beighton, Henry (d. 1743), FRS 1720. Surveyor and engineer; mapmaker. Contributed to the development of the steam engine. [DNB]

Birchensha, John (d. 1681). Music theorist and composer. Composed fantasies, airs, suites, etc. Wrote on the mathematical relationship of tones and on temperament. [NG]

Blondeau, Pierre (fl. 1747-76). [Possible author of item I-81.] Sculptor, professor at the Académie de Saint Luc. Active in Paris and Lyon. [IBNH]

Boccone, Paolo (1633-1703 or 1704). Publications in French, Italian, and Latin on plants and therapy. [EI; NUC, d. 1703]

Boyle, Robert (1627-91), FRS 1660. Experimental physicist, chemist, natural philosopher. Wrote on science, philosophy, theology, pneumatics; published significant discoveries on the nature of air, including experiments on sound. Also wrote on heat and cold and on theories about color. Advocated mechanistic theory of matter and rational, theoretical approach to chemistry. [DSB]

Brocklesby, Richard (1722-97), FRS 1746/7. Physician. Among his publications are *Reflections on Ancient and Modern Music, with the Application to the Cure of Diseases . . .* , 1749, and *Oeconomical and Medical Observations . . .* , 1764, which discussed principles of hygiene. Great uncle of Thomas Young (see below). [DNB]

Brouncker, William (1620?-84), FRS 1660. Second viscount Brouncker; first president of Royal Society (1662-77). Literary work and contributions to mathematics. Held various government positions. Published translation of Descartes' *Musical Compendium* with his own criticism. President of

Gresham College 1664-67. [DNB]

Bruce, Alexander (ca. 1629-80), FRS 1660. Second Earl of Kincardine. [DNB]

Bruni, Giuseppe Lorenzo (d. 1775), FRS 1743/4. Anatomist. Professor of anatomy at the University of Turin. [Pogg]

Brydone, Patrick (1736-1818), FRS 1773. Traveller and author; experiments in electricity. [DNB]

Burney, Charles (1726-1814), FRS 1773. Composer and music historian. Wrote a history of music and descriptions of his travels in France, Italy, Germany, and the Netherlands. [NG]

Byrom, John (1692-1763), FRS 1723/4. Poet and stenographer. Invented a new system of shorthand. [DNB]

Carlisle, Anthony (1768-1840), FRS 1804. Physician and surgeon; pupil of Hunter (see below). Invented modifications to surgical tools; performed experiments on electricity. Papers on anatomical, surgical topics. Croonian lecturer, 1805 and 1806. [DSB]

Carrillo, Josephi Israel (fl. 1728). Physician to the king of Tunis. Native of Madrid.

Cavallo, Tiberius (1749-1809), FRS 1779. Physicist; experiments in electricity, magnetism; amateur violinist. Published treatises on electricity, on the nature of air, and on natural philosophy (including a text on the physics of music). [DSB]

Charas, Moyse (1619-98). Physician and chemist. Treatises on snake poisons and pharmacology. Member Académie Royale des Sciences. [GDEL, DHF]

Charleton, Walter (1620-1707), FRS 1661. Physician, natural philosopher. Writings on medicine, physiology. Published *Physiologia* . . . (1654), based on Gassendi; exponent of atomic philosophy. Also wrote on theories of Stonehenge. [DSB]

Chaulet, Colet de (fl. 1745). Anatomist. Student of François Jos. Hunauld (1701-42), FRS, who was professor of anatomy at the Jardin du Roi in Paris and a member of the Académie Royale des Sciences.

Cirillo, Domenico (1739-99). Botanist, zoologist, physician. Professor of botany, University of Naples. [EI]

Cleland, Archibald (fl. 1739-48). Surgeon to General [George] Wade's Regiment of Horse. Later, surgeon at the general hospital in the city of Bath. Proposed as candidate to R.S., March 1739 (rejected). [BLC]

Conyers, John (1644-1719). Apothecary and amateur instrument maker. Began work entitled, "Magneticall Mistery Explained . . . . " [Arm, Hunt, Tay]

Cooper, Astley Paston (1768-1841), FRS 1802. Surgeon, anatomist. Copley medal for work on the ear; numerous publications on anatomy and surgical techniques. [DNB]

Cordié, J. de (fl. 1734).

Cornelio, Tomasso (1614-84?). Physician, philosopher, and mathematician. Professor of theoretical medicine in Naples. Published *Progymnasmata physica* (1663). [Old, J, NUC]

Court de Gebelin, Antoine (1725-84). Member of the Royal Academy of Rochelle and the Economic Society of Bern. Studies in mythology, etymology, animal magnetism, universal grammar. [J, NBU]

Creed (d. ca. 1747). London clergyman. [Sch]

Croke [Crook], George (d. 1680), FRS 1676/7. High sheriff of Oxfordshire, 1664ff. Professor of rhetoric at Gresham College. [Old]

Davis, John (fl. 1684-85). Minister of Little Leak in Nottinghamshire. [Gun]

Derham, William (1657-1735), FRS 1702/3. Contributions in natural history and theology. Vicar of Upminster and other ecclesiastic posts. Published books on theology and papers on meteorology, astronomy, and natural history. Edited works of Robert Hooke and John Ray. [DSB]

Desagulliers, John Theophilus (1683-1744), FRS 1714. Experimental natural philosopher. Furnished experiments for Royal Society. Copley medal 1734, 1736, and 1741. Over 50 papers in the *Philosophical Transactions* on optics, mechanics, electricity, and improvements to various scientific instruments. [DSB]

Descartes, René (1596-1650). Mathematician and philosopher. The "father of modern philosophy." Pursued a unitary universal science; theories on separation between mind and body (nature). Influential publications including: *Discourse on Method* (1637) and *Principles of Philosophy* (1644). [Brit]

Desgabetz [-bets], Robert (1620-78). French Benedictine. Disciple of Descartes, whose principles he applied to theological studies. [GLE]

D'estrehan [D'estreseau], see d'Estrehan.

Diemerbroeck, Isbando de (1609-74). Professor of anatomy and medicine at Utrecht. [Old]

Doddridge, Philip? (1702-51). Minister. Wrote hymns and religious works. [DNB]

Dodington [Dorrington?], John (d. 1673). Secretary to Thomas Belasyse, Viscount Fauconberg, on diplomatic mission to Venice. Resident of Venice. [Old]

Douglas, James (1675-1742), FRS 1706. Physician and anatomist. Numerous publications in anatomy and botany, including a general bibliography on anatomy. Physician to the queen. [DNB]

Du Hamel, Jean-Baptiste (1623-1706). Anatomist, priest. Secretary of Académie Royale des Sciences, 1666-97. [DSB]

Du Quet (fl. 1706-21). Engineer and inventor. Various inventions approved by the Académie Royale des Sciences and published in its *Machines et inventions*. (PT index gives first name as Andrew). [New]

Du Verney, Joseph-Guichard (1648-1730). Physician. Professor of anatomy at the Jardin du Roi. His principle work, *Traité de l'organe de l'ouie* (1683), gave the first exact description of the structure of the inner ear. Member of Académie Royale des Sciences. [GDEL, DSB]

Ellis, Henry (1721-1806), FRS 1749/50. Traveller, hydrographer and colonial governor. Expedition to seek Northwest passage, 1746-47; published narrative of travels. Governor of Georgia and Nova Scotia. [DNB]

d'Estrehan [possibly d'Estreseau] (fl. 1669). Resident of Caen.

Evelyn, John (1620-1706), FRS 1660 (proposed). Horticulturalist. Various governmental appointments. His book on cultivation of timber trees *(Sylva)* was the first book to be published by the R.S. He also published a translation of Lucretius' *De rerum natura* and a commentary on Gassendi. [DSB]

Eyles-Stiles, Francis Haskins (d. 1762), FRS 1742/3. Third Baronet of Gidea Hall, Havering, Essex. Commissioner of Victualling (navy post).

Travelled to Naples after 1760. Burney and Hawkins both praise his article on the Greek modes. [GEC Bar]

Felici [Felice], Giovanni Battista [John Baptist] (fl. 1717-39). Wrote "Annales provinciae S. Josephi . . . ," Vienna 1739; publications on use of chocolate, 1728. [J, BLC]

Franklin, Benjamin (1706-90), FRS 1756. American printer, author, diplomat, philosopher, and scientist. Founded the precursor to the American Philosophical Society and the first public library. Significant experiments and publications in electricity. Also invented glass harmonica. Copley medal, 1753. [Brit]

Freeman, William (d. 1750), FRS 1735. (Author of item X-87; author of I-52/IV-10 appears to be a different person.) [Bull]

Freke, John (1688-1756), FRS 1729. Surgeon to St. Bartholomew's Hospital. [DNB]

Gaubil, Antoine (1689-1759). French Jesuit. Interpreter at court of Peking for over 30 years. Wrote on astronomy, geography, history, and literature of China. [GLE]

Gebelin, Antoine Court de, see Court de Gebelin, Antoine.

Geekie, Alexander (d.1761?), FRS 1710. Surgeon. [Bull]

Goddard, Jonathan (ca. 1617-75), FRS 1660. Physician. Gresham professor of physic; warden of Merton College, Oxford. Performed numerous experiments for R.S. Published articles and essays on "physick." [DNB, Bir]

Grandi, Guido (1671-1742), FRS 1709. Mathematician; professor of philosophy and mathematics at Pisa. Voluminous scientific correspondence. Published theoretical works and textbooks in math. [DSB]

Gray, James (d. 1773). Diplomat and antiquary. Envoy extraordinary to King of Naples, 1753ff; later minister plenipotentiary to King of Spain. One of original founders of Society of Dilettanti (1732). [DNB Supp]

Gregory, David (1661-1708), FRS 1692. Astronomer. Held chair of mathematics at University of Edinburgh; later, Savilian professor of astronomy at Oxford. Publications in mathematics and astronomy;

produced edition of works of Euclid. [DNB]

Guthrie, Mathew (d. 1807), FRS 1782. Physician of the Imperial Corps of Noble Cadets in St. Petersburg. Wrote book on Russian antiquities and edited travels of his wife. [Bull, Walis]

Hadley, John (1682-1744), FRS 1716/17. Mathematician; work in mechanics. Improved reflecting telescope; invented reflecting quadrant. [DNB]

Halley, Edmund (1656-1742), FRS 1678. Astronomer and mathematician. First to calculate orbit of a comet. Published papers on diverse scientific topics. [Brit]

Hamilton, James (1686-1744), FRS 1715. Lord Paisley, 7th Earl of Abercorn. Author of work on magnetism; possible joint author with Pepusch of *Treatise on Harmony.* [DNB]

Hamilton, James (1712-89). Eighth Earl of Abercorn. Son of above. [DNB]

Hansch, Michael Gottlieb (1683-1749). Lived in Leipzig. Acquired Kepler's manuscripts, had them bound, and published part of the letters in them. [Old, NUC, C]

Harris, John (1666?-1719), FRS 1696. Writer, divine, topographer. Various ecclesiatical posts. Prepared first English "Dictionary of Arts and Sciences." Other publications on theology, mathematics, astronomy, history, etc. [DNB]

Hauksbee, Francis [the elder] (d. 1713?), FRS 1705. Experiments and discoveries in electricity. Contrived first electrical machine. Published *Physico-Mechanical Experiments,* 1709. [DNB]

Hautefeuille, Jean de (1647-1724), FRS 1687. Physician and mechanician. Inventions in clockwork. Publications on clocks, pendulum mechanisms, speaking trumpet, etc. [NBU]

Heisig [Hessack?] (fl. 1681). "A Swedish gentleman."

Herbert, John (d. after 1706), FRS 1677. Vice-president of R.S. in 1703. [HunR]

Hevelius, Johann (1611-87), FRS 1664. Astronomer. Compiled atlas of the moon, catalog of stars, and celestial atlas. [Brit]

Hill, Abraham (1635-1721), FRS 1660. Treasurer R.S. for many years. Wrote biography of Isaac Barrow. Miscellaneous correspondence and papers housed in British Library. [DNB]

Hillyer [Hillier], J[ames?] (fl. 1688). [Alli]

Holder, William (1616-98), FRS 1661. Mathematician, musician, divine. Held various ecclesiatical posts. Subdean of Chapel Royal. Composed anthems, evening service. Wrote *Treatise of Natural Grounds of Harmony* (1694). [NG]

Home, Everard (1756-1832), FRS 1787. Surgeon. Student and assistant of John Hunter (see below). Lecturer on anatomy and surgeon at St. George's Hospital. Often delivered Croonian lecture at Royal Society. Over 100 papers published in *Philosophical Transactions* and elsewhere. Destroyed many of Hunter's papers after allegedly using them to prepare his own works on anatomy. Copley medal 1807. [DNB]

Hooke, Robert (1635-1703), FRS 1663. Physicist. Research in a wide variety of scientific fields. Discovered law of elasticity ("Hooke's Law"). Assistant to Robert Boyle in development of air pump. Curator of experiments for the R.S.; secretary, 1677-82. Published *Micrographia* (1665). [Brit]

Hoskins [Hoskyns], John (1634-1705), FRS 1661. Baronet of Harewood and Morehampton Park, Herefordshire. Non-practicing lawyer. MP for Herefordshire, but took no active part in politics. President of Royal Society 1682-83, secretary 1685-87. [DNB]

Hunt, Henry (fl. 1681-1710). Operator to the Royal Society. [Gun]

Hunter, John (1728-93), FRS 1767. Anatomist and surgeon. First to have introduced to England many basic principles of surgery. Delivered Croonian lecture 6 times; Copley medal, 1787. Surgeon at St. George's Hospital and surgeon extraordinary to George III. Numerous papers and other publications including a treatise on the blood, inflammation, and gunshot wounds. [DNB]

Huntington, Robert (1637-1701). Orientalist and bishop of Raphoe. Provost of Trinity College, Dublin 1683-92. Collected numerous manuscripts from the East. [DNB]

Huygens, Christiaan (1629-95), FRS 1663. Mathematician, astronomer, physician. Founded wave theory of light; discovered shape of Saturn's rings; studies in dynamics. One of founders of Académie Royale des

Sciences, 1666. [Brit]

Jenner, Edward (1749-1823), FRS 1789. Surgeon. Discovered process of vaccination. Student of John Hunter (see above). Also an amateur musician (violinist). [DNB, Brit]

Justel, Henri (1620-93), FRS 1681. Librarian. Born in Paris; secretary to Louis XIV. Emigrated to England, 1681. Appointed by Charles II as keeper of king's library at St. James. [DNB]

Kircher, Athanasius (1601-80). German historian, theologian, and music theorist. Academic positions at University of Wurzburg, Avignon, Collegio Romano. Published treatises on mathematics, physics, and music theory, including *Musurgia universalis* (1650). [NG]

Kirkby, Christopher (fl. 1668-74). Tradesman. Recorded as sailing from England to Danzig in 1668. [Old]

Klein, Jacob Theodore (1685-1759), FRS 1728/9. Zoologist. Court secretary in Danzig. Published about 25 studies on various animals, including an important work on sea urchins. [DSB]

La Condamine, Charles-Marie de (1701-74), FRS 1748. Mathematician, naturalist. Member Académie Royale des Sciences (1730). Participated in scientific exploratory expeditions, including one to Peru sponsored by the academy, which was designed to verify Newton's theory of the flattening of the earth at the poles. Published books relating to his travels, as well as numerous articles. [DSB]

Le Cat, Claude-Nicolas (1700-68), FRS 1739/40. Physician, surgeon, anatomist. Chief surgeon at Hotel-Dieu in Rouen. Invented or perfected several instruments in lithotomy. Published *Traité des sens*. One of founding members of Rouen Académie des Sciences. [DSB]

Lewis, George (d. 1729). Priest. Perhaps chaplain to East India Co. at Fort St. George. May have been Archdeacon of Meath and rector of Kells, 1723-29. [AC]

Lister, Martin (1638?-1712), FRS 1671. Zoologist and physician. Practiced medicine in York. Published articles and other works on zoology, botany, meteorology, minerals, antiquities, medicine, etc. Significant treatise on shells. [DNB]

Lhuyd [Lloyd], Edward (1660-1709), FRS 1708. Celtic scholar and naturalist. Keeper of Ashmolean Museum. Investigations of antiquities and archeology. Published *Archaeologia Britannica . . .* (1707). [DNB]

Long, Roger (1680-1770). [Possible author of item X-69.] Astronomer and cleric. Held chair in astronomy and geometry at Cambridge. Published works on astronomy and "the Music Speech, Spoken at the Public Commencement in Cambridge," 1714. [DNB]

Mariotte, Edme (d. 1684). Experimental physicist. Credited with introducing experimental physics into France. Central figure in Paris Académie Royale des Sciences. Proved many theories of others through careful experimental work. Published books on optics, on impact of bodies, on pneumatic and hydraulic experiments, etc. [DSB]

Marsh, Narcissus (1638-1713). Bishop and archbishop of Ireland (bp. of Ferns and Leighlin; archbp. of Cashel and bp. of Emly; archbp. of Dublin and bp. of Glendalough; archbp. of Armagh). Provost of Trinity College, Dublin (1679). Aided Boyle in preparation of Irish translation of Old Testament. One of founders of Royal Dublin Society. [DNB]

McLaurin, Colin (1698-1746), FRS 1719. Mathematician and natural philosopher. Professorial appointments at Aberdeen and Edinburgh. Wrote important *mémoire* on the percussion of bodies. [DNB]

Mead, Richard (1673-1754), FRS 1703. Physician. Wrote important treatise on poisons. Physician at St. Thomas's Hospital and physician to George II. Edited various medical works. [DNB]

Mengoli, Pietro (1626-86). Bolognese mathematician. Parish priest and prior of the church of Santa Maria Maddalena. Significant publications in mathematics; also wrote *Speculazioni di musica* (1670). [EI]

Miles, Henry (1698-1763), FRS 1743. Minister and scientific writer. Published papers on natural history, meteorology and electricity in *Philosophical Transactions*. Aided Birch in preparation of the works of Boyle. [DNB]

Milliet de Chales, Claude François (1621-78). Mathematician. Professeur royal d'hydrographie at Marseille. [DHF]

Molinetti, Antonio (d. 1673). Professor of anatomy and theoretical medicine at University of Padua. Publications in anatomy. [EUI]

Molyneux, Thomas (1661-1733), FRS 1686. Physician. Published various papers in the *Transactions* on medicine, anatomy, zoology, etc. Professor of medicine at University of Dublin. [DNB]

Molyneux, William (1656-98), FRS 1685/6. Philosopher, applied mathematician. Brother of Thomas (above). One of founders and first secretary of Dublin Philosophical Society. Published treatise on optics (1692). [DNB]

Moray [Murray], Robert (1608-1673), FRS 1660. Statesman and military officer. One of the founders of the Royal Society and its president for the year before incorporation. Administrative duties in Scotland; also had musical interests. [DNB]

Morhof, Daniel George (1639-91). Writer and translator. Professor of poetry at Rostock; professor of history at Kiel. [Old]

Morland, Samuel (1625-95). Diplomat, mathematician, inventor. Performed experiments in hydrostatics and hydraulics. Invented the speaking trumpet, arithmetical machines, perpetual almanac, improvements to fire engines, and a water pump. Performed significant experiments leading toward the development of the steam engine. [DNB]

Moulin [Molines, Mullen], Allen (d. 1690), FRS 1683. Anatomist. Prominent member Dublin Philosophical Society, at which he presented papers on human and comparative anatomy. Publications in the field, including a treatise on the anatomy of the elephant. [DNB]

Musgrave, William (1655?-1721), FRS 1683/4. Physician and antiquary. Secretary of the Royal Society and editor of *Philosophical Transactions* (1685). Aided formation of scientific society in Oxford. Publications on medical topics and antiquities. [DNB]

Nesbitt [Nisbet], Robert (d. 1761), FRS 1725. Physician. Publications on human osteogeny. [Bull, DNB]

Nevill, Francis (fl. 1712). Published antiquarian papers in PT. [Alli]

Newton, Isaac (1642-1727), FRS 1671/2. Physicist and mathematician. "Culminating figure of the 17th century scientific revolution." Discovered composition of white light; formulated three fundamental laws of mechanics, leading to law of gravity; invented the infinitesimal calculus. Influential publications including *Opticks* (1704) and *Principia* (1687), as well as numerous articles. President of R.S. 1703-27. [Brit]

Nicholson, Henry (d. 1723), FRS 1716. Physician in Leyden and Dublin. [Bull]

Nixon, John (d. 1777), FRS 1744. Rector of Cold Higham, Northamptonshire. [Bull, Gent M]

North, Francis (1637-85). Lawyer, amateur musician. Lord Keeper of the Great Seal under Charles II. His *Philosophical Essay of Musick* (1677) discusses harmony in the spirit of new scientific discoveries. [NG]

Oldenburg, Henry (ca. 1618-1677), FRS 1660. Natural philosopher. Born in Bremen. Emigrated to England ca. 1640. First secretary of Royal Society. Founded *Philosophical Transactions*. Maintained a voluminous scientific correspondence. Published papers and translations of scientific work. (Sometimes signed his name as "Grubendol.") [DNB]

Pache, S. (fl. 1676). From Caen.

Paderni, Camillo (d. ca. 1770), FRS 1755. Keeper of the museum at Herculaneum. [NUC]

Paisley, James Lord, Earl of Abercorn, see Hamilton, James.

Papin, Denis (1647-ca. 1712), FRS 1680? Physicist. Invented pressure cooker and conceived basic ideas for steam engine. Assistant to Huygens for the air pump; worked with Robert Boyle. [HunR, Brit]

Pardies, Ignace Gaston (1636-73). Physicist; French Jesuit priest. Taught at Bordeaux, La Rochelle, and the College Clermont in Paris. Published treatises on physics and geometry. Important correspondence with Newton, et al. [DSB]

Parsons, James (1705-70), FRS 1741. Physician and antiquary. Also a flute player. Physician to public infirmary of St. Giles. Publications in anatomy and medicine. [DNB]

Pearson, George (1751-1828), FRS 1791. Physician and chemist. Published *Observations and Experiments . . . [on] the Springs of Buxton* (1784), showing that the gas from the springs was nitrogen. Physician to St.

George's Hospital and to the Duke of York's household. Performed experiments in chemistry and promoted use of vaccination. Publications on chemical topics. [DNB]

Pepusch, John Christopher (1667-1752), FRS 1745. Composer and theorist. Born in Germany; employed at Prussian court. Emigrated to England at the end of the seventeenth century. Music director to James Brydges, Duke of Chandos, 1713-ca.1730. Composed theatre music (including arrangements in the *Beggar's Opera)*, sonatas, church music, cantatas. Wrote treatise on music, 1730 and 1731. [NG]

Petty, William (1623-87), FRS 1660. Political economist. One of founders of Royal Society. Professor of anatomy at Brasenose College; physician-general to army in Ireland. Performed significant surveying work in Ireland. Published papers on mechanics and practical inventions; writings on political economy. [DNB]

Platt, Thomas (fl. 1672-73). The only biographical information on Platt is found in a letter from Thomas Derham to Joseph Williamson, recommending Platt for appointment as a secretary. He was said to be master of several languages and to be in the high esteem of the Duke of Tuscany (see Old. no. 2038). [Old]

Plot, Robert (1640-96), FRS 1677. Antiquary. Wrote *The Natural History of Oxfordshire* . . . (1676) and other similar works. Professor of chemistry at Oxford; first custos of Ashmolean Museum. Secretary of R.S. 1682-84; edited *Philosophical Transactions,* vols. 13 and 14. [DNB]

Pococke, Richard (1704-65), FRS 1741/2. Bishop in Ireland (Ossory, Meath). Travelled widely and published an account of his journeys to the East. [Bull, DNB]

Pope, Walter (d. 1714), FRS 1661. Astronomer. Professor of astronomy at Gresham College 1660-87. [DNB]

Powle, Henry (1630-92), FRS 1660? Politician. Represented Cirencester or East Grinstead in parliament beginning in 1670. Master of the rolls and speaker of the Convention parliament. Member of privy council, 1678 and 1688. [DNB]

Rameau, Jean Philippe (1683-1764). French composer and theorist. Wrote significant treatises on music theory, including *Traité de l'harmonie* (1722), a landmark in the development of tonal theory. Composed numerous operas and other vocal works, keyboard compositions, etc. [NG]

Ray [Wray], John (1627-1705), FRS 1667. Botanist and zoologist. Published catalogs of plants; made significant strides in botanical classification. Also worked on classification of insects and edited the zoological works of Willughby. [DNB]

Roach, Richard (1662-1730). Rector of St. Augustine's, Hackney. [DNB]

Robartes [Roberts], Francis (1650?-1718), FRS 1673. Politician and musician. Member of parliament 1672ff. [DNB]

Rooke, Lawrence (1622-62), FRS 1660. Astronomer. Professor of astronomy, and later of geometry, at Gresham College. Published articles on astronomony and other scientific topics. [DNB]

Rose, Alexander (d. ca. 1770). Capt., 52nd regiment.

Rutty, William (1687-1730), FRS 1720. Physician. Published *A Treatise of the Urinary Passages* (1726). Secretary of R.S. 1727-30. Edited *Philosophical Transactions*, vol. 35. [DNB]

Salmon, Thomas (1648-1706). Music theorist, amateur musician, clergyman. His *Essay to the Advancement of Musick* (1672) suggested notational reforms and his *Proposal to Perform Music in Mathematical Proportions* (1688) presented a method for creating acoustically pure intervals on the viol. [NG]

Sengwerdius, Wolferdus (1646-1724). Philos. Professor Ordinarius and Bibliothecarius in Leiden. Wrote tract on the tarantula. [J, NUC]

Shadwell, John (1671-1747), FRS 1701. Physician in ordinary to Anne, George I, and George II. [DNB]

Sloane, Hans (1660-1753), FRS 1684/5. Physician, botanist, naturalist. President R.S. 1727-41. Published catalog of plants. Bequeath of his collection of books, manuscripts, and specimens formed basis for British Museum. [DNB]

Smyth, Edward (1665-1720), FRS 1696. Bishop of Down and Connor and other ecclesiatical posts. Member of Irish privy council. Vice-chancellor of

Dublin University. Secretary of Dublin Society (1686). [Hop]

Southwell, Robert (1635-1702), FRS 1662. Diplomat. Envoy to Portugal, Brussels, Brandenburg. Member of parliament. Principal secretary of state for Ireland. President R.S. 1690-95. [DNB, NG]

Steele, Joshua (1700-91). Writer on prosody. Published *An Essay towards Establishing the Melody and Measure of Speech* . . . (1775), in which he proposed a method of notation for speech similar to that for musical sounds. Resided in Barbados from 1780. [DNB, NG]

Steigertahl, Johann Georg (b. ca. 1667), FRS 1714. Physician to George I. Resided in England 1714-ca. 1727. [Munk, NUC]

Stiles, Francis Haskins Eyles, see Eyles-Stiles.

Tasman, Abel Janszoon (1603?-59). Dutch navigator and explorer. Discovered Tasmania, New Zealand, Tonga, and the Fiji Islands. [Brit]

Taylor, Brook (1685-1731), FRS 1711/12. Mathematician and amateur musician. Published significant paper on vibrations in strings, as well as the treatise *Methodus incrementorum directa et inversa* (1715) and other works. Secretary R.S. 1714-18. [NG]

Thornycroft, Edward (fl. 1705). [Alli]

Turberville, Daubeney [Daubigny] (1612-96). Physician; specialist in eye diseases. [DNB]

Tyson, Edward (1650-1708), FRS 1679. Physician to Bridewell and Bethlehem hospitals. Lecturer to the Barber-Surgeons. Published medical case studies and monographs on various animals including the porpoise, the rattlesnake, the tapeworm, the opossum, etc. [DNB, Munk]

Valsalva, Antonio Maria (1666-1723). Anatomist and surgeon. Lecturer in anatomy in Bologna. Surgeon at hospital of S. Orsola. Published anatomical studies on the ear, the aorta, etc. Most important work is *De aure humano* (Bologna, 1704). [EI]

Vaucancon, Jacques de (1709-82). Inventor. Built automatons; invented important machine tools; automated the loom. Member of Académie Royale des Sciences. [Brit]

Vernon, Francis (1637?-77), FRS 1672. Traveler and author. Traveled in

Sweden, France, Greece, Italy, Persia. Secretary to embassy in Paris. Served as medium of communication between French and English scientists for many years. [DNB]

Vieussens, Raymond (1641-1715), FRS 1688. Anatomist, physician. Chief physician at Hotel Dieu St.-Eloi (leading hospital of Montpellier). Published books on nervous system, the heart, and on fermentation. Member Académie Royale des Sciences (1699). [DSB]

Viviani, Vincenzo (1622-1703), FRS 1696. Mathematician. Student of Galileo; member Accademia del Cimento and Académie Royale des Sciences. Studied mathematics of the Greeks; reconstructed and translated Greek treatises. [DSB]

Volta, Alessandro Giuseppe Antonio Anastasio (1745-1827), FRS 1791. Physicist. Invented the electric battery; isolated methane gas. Professor of physics University of Pavia. Copley medal, 1794. [Brit]

Vossius, Isaac (1618-89), FRS 1664. Canon of Windsor, Dutch scholar (original name: Vos). Teacher of Queen Christina of Stockholm. Emigrated to England in 1670. Writings on theology, chronology, scientific matters. Published *De Poematum cantu et viribus rythmi* (1673), which advocates strong links between poetry and music. [DNB]

Walker, Joshua (ca. 1655-1705). Rector of Great Billing, Northants. [Fos, Hunt]

Waller, Richard (c. 1646-c.1714), FRS 1681. Bachelor's degree at Cambridge, 1667. Secretary of Royal Society, 1687ff. Edited *Philosophical Transactions*, vols. 17 and 18. [Old]

Wallis, John (1616-1703), FRS 1661. Mathematician. Contributions to origins of calculus. Publications in mathematics and mechanics. [DNB]

Wanley, Humfrey (1672-1726), FRS 1706. Antiquary. Assistant in Bodleian Library. Compiled various manuscript catalogs. Secretary of Society for Promoting Christian Knowledge. [DNB]

Wathan, Jonathan (fl. 1763-92). [NUC]

Watson, William (1715-87), FRS 1741. Physician, naturalist. Published significant works on electricity. More than 50 original papers and summaries of the work of others printed in the *Philosophical Transactions*. Also published papers on botany, chemistry. Copley medal, 1745. [DNB]

Wilkins, Charles (1749 or 50-1836), FRS 1788. Orientalist. Superintendant of East India Company's factories at Maldah (Bengal). Founded, with Sir William Jones, the Asiatic Society of Bengal. Later, librarian for East India Co. Published articles on Indian epigraphy and translations from Sanskrit. Also, grammatical works on Sanskrit; catalogs of Jones' manuscripts. [DNB]

Wilkins, John (1614-72), FRS 1660. Bishop of Chester. Warden of Wadham College; later, master of Trinity College, Cambridge. Published religious writings. [DNB, Bir]

Wotton, William (1666-1727), FRS 1687. Scholar. Child prodigy in area of languages. Published *Reflections upon Ancient and Modern Learning* (1694), which summarized discoveries in nature and physical science. Also writings on the ancients. [DNB]

Wren, Christopher (1632-1723), FRS 1660. Architect, astronomer, mathematician. Designed over 50 London churches, as well as other buildings. Professor of astronomy at Gresham College and Oxford. [DNB, Bir]

Wynde [Winde, Wynne, Wind], William (d. 1722), FRS 1662. Architect and military officer. Designed English country houses. [BA]

Young, Thomas (1773-1829), FRS 1794. Physician, physicist, Egyptologist. Professor of natural philosophy, Royal Institution, 1801-03; physician to St. George's Hospital, 1811ff.; foreign secretary of Royal Society, 1804ff. Established principle of interference of light and wave theory of light. Made significant discoveries in the anatomy of the eye (changes in lens shape, cause of astigmatism, etc.) and in optics (including work on color, on polarization, etc.). Helped decipher the Rosetta stone. Also other work in physics, including measuring size of molecules, surface tension in liquids, etc. Amateur musician (flutist). [Brit, DNB]

SELECTED BIBLIOGRAPHY

Allibone, Samuel Austin. *A Critical Dictionary of English Literature and British and American Authors*. Philadelphia: J. B. Lippincott Co., 1891.

Anderson, Warren. *Ethos and Education in Greek Music*. Cambridge: Harvard University Press, 1966.

Andrade, E. N. da C. *A Brief History of the Royal Society*. London: Royal Society, 1960.

Armytage, W. H. G. "The Royal Society and the Apothecaries." *Notes and Records of the Royal Society* 11 (1954): 22-37.

Atcherson, W. T. "Seventeenth-Century Music Theory: England." *Journal of Music Theory* 16 (1972): 6-15.

Aubrey, John. *Brief Lives and Other Selected Writings*. Ed. Anthony Powell. London: Cresset Press, 1949.

Birch, Thomas. *History of the Royal Society of London*. London: 1756-57. Reprint, ed. A. Rupert and Marie Boas Hall. New York and London: Johnson Reprint Corp., 1968.

Boyle, Robert. *The Works of the Honourable Robert Boyle*. Edited by Thomas Birch. London: 1744. Reprint of the 1772 ed., ed. Douglas McKie. Hildesheim: G. Olms, 1965-66.

Brasch, Frederick E. *The Royal Society of London and Its Influence upon Scientific Thought in the American Colonies*. Reprint from *Scientific Monthly* 33 (Oct./Nov. 1931).

Burney, Charles. *A General History of Music, from the Earliest Ages to the*

Present Period. 2nd ed., 1789. Reprint, ed. Frank Mercer, New York: Dover Publications, 1957.

Caspar, Max. *Kepler.* London and New York: Abelard-Schuman, 1959.

Chenette, Louis F. "Music Theory in the British Isles during the Enlightenment." Ph.D. dissertation, Ohio State University, 1967.

Cockayne, G. E., ed. *Complete Baronetage.* Exeter: William Pollard and Co., 1906.

Cockayne, G. E., ed. *Complete Peerage.* London: 1910-59.

Cohen, Albert. *Music in the French Academy of Sciences.* Princeton: Princeton University Press, 1981.

Cohen, Albert. "A Study of Instrumental Practice in Seventeenth-Century France." *Galpin Society Journal* 15 (1962): 3-17.

Cohen, Albert, and Leta E. Miller. *Music in the Paris Academy of Sciences, 1666-1793.* Detroit Studies in Music Bibliography, 43. Detroit: Information Coordinators, 1979.

Cohen, H. F. "Christiaan Huygens on Consonance and the Division of the Octave." In *Studies on Christiaan Huygens,* ed. Bos, et al. Lisse: Swets and Zeitlinger, 1980.

Colvin, Howard. *A Biographical Dictionary of British Architects, 1600-1840.* London: John Murray, 1978.

Crone, John. *A Concise Dictionary of Irish Biography.* London: Longmans, Green and Co., 1928.

Dostrovsky, Sigalia. "The Origins of Vibration Theory: the Scientific Revolution and the Nature of Music." Ph.D. dissertation, Princeton University, 1969.

Evelyn, John. *The Diary of John Evelyn.* Ed. E. S. de Beer. Oxford: Clarendon Press, 1955.

Foster, Joseph. *Alumni Oxonienses: The Members of the University of Oxford.* Oxford, 1891-92. Reprint, Liechtenstein: Kraus Reprint, 1968.

Gouk, Penelope. "Acoustics in the Early Royal Society 1660-1680." *Notes and Records of the Royal Society* 36 (1982): 155-75.

Gouk, Penelope. "Music in the Natural Philosophy of the Early Royal Society." Ph.D. dissertation, Warburg Institute, 1982.

Gouk, Penelope. "The Role of Acoustics and Music Theory in the Scientific

Work of Robert Hooke." *Annals of Science* 37 (1980): 573-605.

Green, Burdette Lamar. "The Harmonic Series from Mersenne to Rameau: An Historical Study of Circumstances Leading to Its Recognition and Application to Music." Ph.D. dissertation, Ohio State University, 1969.

Grew, Nehemiah. *Musaeum Regalis Societatis or a Catalogue and Description of the Natural and Artificial Rarities Belonging to the Royal Society and Preserved at Gresham Colledge.* London, 1681.

Gunther, Robert William Theodore. *Early Science in Oxford.* Oxford, 1920ff. Reprint, London: Dawsons, 1967ff.

Hahn, Roger. *The Anatomy of a Scientific Institution: The Paris Academy of Sciences 1666-1803.* Berkeley: University of California Press, 1971.

Halley, Edmond. *Correspondence and Papers of Edmond [sic] Halley.* Ed. Eugene Fairfield MacPike. Oxford: Clarendon Press, 1932.

Hawkins, John. *A General History of the Science and Practice of Music.* London, 1776. Reprint, with introduction by Charles Cudworth, New York: Dover Publications, 1963.

Haydn, Joseph Timothy. *The Book of Dignities.* Baltimore: Genealogical Publishing Co., 1970.

Hooke, Robert. *The Posthumous Works of Robert Hooke.* Ed. Richard Waller. London, 1705. Reprint, ed. T. M. Brown, New York and London: F. Cass, 1971.

Hoppin, K. T. "The Royal Society and Ireland." *Notes and Records of the Royal Society* 20 (1965): 78-99.

Hunt, Frederick. *Origins in Acoustics.* New Haven and London: Yale University Press, 1978.

Hunter, Michael. *John Aubrey and the Realm of Learning.* London: Duckworth, 1975.

Hunter, Michael. *The Royal Society and its Fellows, 1660-1700: The Morphology of an Early Scientific Institution.* British Society for the History of Science, 1982.

Hunter, Michael. *Science and Society in Restoration England.* Cambridge: Cambridge University Press, 1981.

Huygens, Christiaan. *Oeuvres complètes.* La Haye: Société Hollandaise des Sciences, 1888-1950.

Kassler, J. C. *The Science of Music in Britain 1714-1830: A Catalogue of Writings, Lectures and Inventions.* New York and London: Garland Publishing, 1979.

Lindsay, R. Bruce. "The Story of Acoustics." In *Acoustics: Historical and Philosophical Development.* Stroudsburg, Pa.: Dowden, Hutchinson and Ross, 1972.

Lloyd, L. S. "Musical Theory in the Early *Philosophical Transactions." Notes and Records of the Royal Society* 3 (1940-41): 149-57.

Lyons, Henry. *The Royal Society 1660-1940: A History of Its Administration under Its Charters.* Cambridge: University Press, 1944.

Maddison, R. E. W. "A Tentative Index of the Correspondence of the Honourable Robert Boyle." *Notes and Records of the Royal Society* 13 (1958): 128-201.

Middleton, W. E. Knowles. *The Experimenters: A Study of the Accademia del Cimento.* London and Baltimore: Johns Hopkins Press, 1971.

Miller, Leta E. "Rameau and the Royal Society: New Letters and Documents." *Music and Letters* 66, no. 1 (January 1985): 19-33.

Munk, William. *The Roll of the Royal College of Physicians of London.* London, 1861.

Newton, Isaac. *The Correspondence of Isaac Newton.* Ed. H. W. Turnbull, et al. Cambridge: University Press, 1959-77.

Oldenburg, Henry. *The Correspondence of Henry Oldenburg.* Ed. A. Rupert and Marie Boas Hall. Madison: University of Wisconsin Press, 1965-77.

Ornstein, Martha. *The Role of Scientific Societies in the Seventeenth Century.* Chicago: University of Chicago Press, 1928. Reprint of 3rd ed., 1938, London: Archon Books, 1963.

Palisca, Claude. "Scientific Empiricism in Musical Thought." In *Seventeenth-Century Science and the Arts,* ed. H. H. Rhys. Princeton: Princeton University Press, 1961.

Pepys, Samuel. *The Diary of Samuel Pepys.* Ed. Robert Latham and William Matthews. Berkeley and Los Angeles: University of California Press, 1970-83.

Poggendorff, Johann Christian. *Biographisch-literarisches Handwörterbuch für Mathematik, Astronomie, Physik* .... Leipzig: J. A. Barth, 1863ff.

Purver, Margery. *The Royal Society: Concept and Creation.* London: Routeledge and Kegan Paul, 1967.

The Record of the Royal Society of London, 4th ed. London: Morrison & Gibb, 1940.

Ruff, Lillian M. "The Seventeenth-Century English Music Theorists." Ph.D. dissertation, Nottingham University, 1962.

Sarton, George. *A Guide to the History of Science.* New York: Ronald Press Company,

Scholes, Percy. *Oxford Companion to Music.* 9th ed. London and New York: Oxford University Press, 1960.

Sigerist, Henry E. "The Story of Tarantism." In *Music and Medicine,* ed. D. M. Schullian and M. Schoen. New York: H. Schuman, 1948.

Sprat, Thomas. *The History of the Royal Society.* London, 1667. Reprint, ed. Jackson I. Cope and Harold Whitmore Jones. St. Louis: Washington University, 1958.

Stimson, Dorothy. *Scientists and Amateurs: A History of the Royal Society.* New York: Schuman, 1948.

Taylor, Eva Germaine Rimington. *The Mathematical Practitioners of Tudor and Stuart England.* Cambridge: University Press, 1954.

Tchen, Ysia. *La musique chinoise en France au XVIIIe siecle.* Paris: Publications Orientalistes de France, 1974.

Truesdell, Clifford A. "The Theory of Aerial Sound, 1687-1788." In *Leonhardi Euleri opera omnia,* ser. 2, vol. 13. Lausanne: Societatis Scientiarum Naturalium Helveticae, 1955.

Truesdell, Clifford A. "The Rational Mechanics of Flexible or Elastic Bodies 1638-1788." In *Leonhardi Euleri opera omnia,* ser. 2, vol. 11, pt. 2. Lausanne: Societatis Scientiarum Naturalium Helveticae, 1955.

Venn, John, ed. *Alumni Cantabrigienses: A Biographical List of All Known Students, Graduates and Holders of Office at the University of Cambridge, from the Earliest Times to 1900.* Cambridge: University Press, 1922-27.

Waliszewski, Kazimierz. *Paul the First of Russia, the Son of Catherine the Great.* Philadelphia: J. B. Lippincott Co., 1913.

Weld, Charles Richard. *A History of the Royal Society.* London: J. W. Parker,

1848. Reprint. New York: Arno Press, 1975.

Wever, Ernest Glen. *The Theory of Hearing.* New York: John Wiley and Sons, 1949.

Wever, Ernest Glen and Merle Lawrence. *Physiological Acoustics.* Princeton: Princeton University Press, 1954.

Wood, Anthony à. *Athenae Oxonienses.* Edited by P. Bliss. London, 1813-20.

Woodcroft, Bennet, ed. *Patents for Inventions.* London: 1871.

INDEXES

Hyphenated numerals refer to catalog items; arabic numbers alone indicate pages.

In Index A, authorship of articles and presentations is indicated by bold-faced references.

In Index B, parenthetical references represent different versions of items cited.

INDEX A: NAMES

INDEX B: SUBJECTS

Spinet, 18, 20, X-69
Tahitian, 24, I-102 (IV-27), X-101
Theorbo, 19
Tongan, 24, I-101, I-102 (IV-27), X-100, X-101
Trumpet, 9, 15, 22, 24, 25, I-33, I-38 (II-49, V-19), I-64, I-116 (IV-35), III-1, III-9 (VI-5, X-6), IV-22, X-70. (See also: Speaking trumpet.)
Trumpet-marine, 9, I-33
Viol, 17, 19, I-56 (III-22), X-65. (See also: archiviole, liraviol.)
Violin, 17, 33, 41, II-42, X-65
Virginal, 17
See also: Otacousticon, Monochord.

Nodes, see Acoustics.
Notation, musical: 16, 39, II-66, X-26; machine for, 20, I-74, X-87; for speech, 44, II-61 (V-31)

Origin of music, III-2
Otacousticon, 21, 25, II-14, II-43, II-62 (V-32), VI-7 (X-18), VIII-5, X-1A, X-20, X-67, X-68, X-74, X-84
See also: Speaking trumpet
Oxford Philosophical Society, I-43, V-10
Organ, see Musical instruments.

Pendulum, use as musical time keeper, 20, X-57
Performances, musical, 17, 19, 41, 42, 45, I-56 (III-22), II-8, X-12, X-13, X-16, X-65
Persian music, I-42 (II-50, V-20)
Philosophical Collections, 47, 48
Pipes from South Seas, see Musical instruments.
Plants, effect of music on, 34-35, II-63 (VI-26), X-77
Poetry and music, see Language and music.
Printing of music, 43, III-17